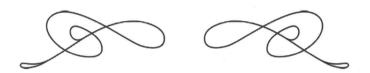

BINGHAMTON WRITES

A Journal of First-Year Writing

Julia Gladstein	Tyler Rock
Yafen Huang	Gabrielle Sagesse
Michael Kotowski	Amanda Samuels
Erick Martinez, Jr.	Mariam Traore
Kasey Muchnicki	Rachel Willison
Evan Neighley	JiaJun Zou
Anita Raychawdhuri	

**Binghamton University,
State University of New York
Eleventh Edition**

HAYDEN
HM
McNEIL

Hayden-McNeil Sustainability

Hayden-McNeil's standard paper stock uses a minimum of 30% post-consumer waste. We offer higher % options by request, including a 100% recycled stock. Additionally, Hayden-McNeil Custom Digital provides authors with the opportunity to convert print products to a digital format. Hayden-McNeil is part of a larger sustainability initiative through Macmillan Higher Ed. Visit http://sustainability.macmillan.com to learn more.

ISBN 978-0-7380-7630-0

Hayden-McNeil Publishing
14903 Pilot Drive
Plymouth, MI 48170
www.hmpublishing.com

Kinney 7630-0 F15-S

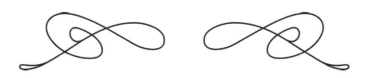

BINGHAMTON WRITES

A Journal of First-Year Writing

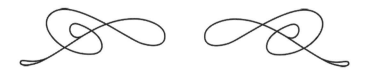

TABLE OF CONTENTS

Introduction

Personal Essays

Op-Eds

Researched Arguments

Writing 110 Essay

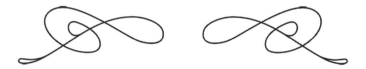

ACKNOWLEDGEMENTS

I'm thankful to the hundreds of Writing 111 students and dozens of Writing 110 students who submitted their best work in the hope of having it selected for *Binghamton Writes*. Thanks first to all of you, and to all the instructors who taught and encouraged you.

I am so grateful to my colleagues who read the submissions, chose the final essays, and then worked with the authors to revise the works in this collection. Jason Allen, Maria Chaves, Trisha Farco, Marcus Heiligenthal, Justin Nevin, Yinka Reed-Nolan, and Matt Salvia joined our editorial team and lent their expertise as Writing 111 instructors and as scholars to this edition. Special thanks to Barret Bowlin for his expert editorial assistance and for working with Melanie J. Cordova, Web Editor, to develop an online presence for *Binghamton Writes*; to Gray Hilmerson, who took on the mammoth task of proofreading the entire work; and of course to Editor-in-Chief Kelly Kinney, whose leadership inspires us all. My deep gratitude to Karen Moroski, Angie Pelekidis, and Jarret Rose, who edited essays for this and previous editions, and to Natalia Andrievskikh, former Writing 111 teacher *par excellence*, who read every single submission and forwarded her recommendations for this and the 10th edition. This year, we offered a prize for the best writing to come out of a Writing 110 class—see the last section of this book—and Sean Fenty, Liam Meilleur, and Paul Shovlin joined me in the tough job of selecting the best from dozens of truly outstanding essays. Liam then went on to work with the winner and runners-up (whose work appears on our website) to edit their work for publication.

We thank Kelly's former colleagues Connie Mick of the University of Notre Dame and Dan Royer of Grand Valley State University for helping to bring the first edition of *Binghamton Writes* to life, and Lad Tobin of Boston College, whose publication of student writing first inspired our own.

Finally, we're glad to acknowledge our heartfelt thanks to our publishers, Hayden-McNeil. Senior Managing Editor Lisa Wess, with her wisdom, generosity, and infinite patience, makes it possible to produce two collections of student writing each year. Thanks also to Hayden-McNeil artist Rachel Huhta and Project Coordinator Lori Hubbard, whose work makes our students' work shine.

Binghamton Writes, Eleventh Edition is dedicated to its authors. JiaJun, Rachel, Mariam, Amanda, Gabrielle, Tyler, Anita, Evan, Kasey, Erick, Michael, Yafen, and Julia: Congratulations from your teachers and supporters.

Wendy Stewart, Lead Editor
Binghamton University, State University of New York

Fall 2015

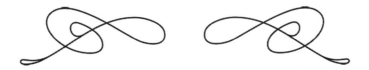

HOW TO USE *BINGHAMTON WRITES:* AN INTRODUCTION FOR STUDENTS AND FACULTY

Binghamton Writes demonstrates how twelve Writing 111 students and one Writing 110 student in the previous academic year have met the challenge of responding to the same prompts you're figuring out right now. Think of these essays not as patterns you should imitate but rather as samples and examples of successful rhetorical choices writers have made.

Within each genre, which essay has the most convincing argument? The most sophisticated analysis? The most effective organization? The most appropriate style? Your answer will be different from some of your classmates', or your fellow teachers'. That's as it should be. Each of us comes to reading—and to writing—with different sensibilities, priorities, and affinities. Each of the Personal Essay writers demonstrate those differences, and yet each succeeds in the task of connecting their own development as individuals with an awareness of playing an active part in something larger than themselves. The Op-Ed writers each take an informed stance on a contemporary social issue, first listening carefully to what other writers are saying, then making their own thoughtful contributions to the discussion. The four Researched Arguments demonstrate how their writers followed up on their own personal interest in diverse topics; what makes these essays scholarly is that they pay close attention to what academics are currently debating in regard to those topics, then situate themselves in relation to those debates.

Study these essays. Talk about them in the classroom. Articulate ways in which all these good essays are different. Think about why you prefer one essay to another. Discuss why a writer might have made a particular rhetorical choice, whether or not that's the choice you would have made. Read the short biographical note preceding each essay: what struggles did these writers work through in addressing the assignment? How are they similar to your own?

And then *on the last day of classes*, once you've revised your essays for your final portfolio, send us one, two, or all three of your own essays. If published, your work will inspire and help future students—and earn you a nice line on a CV, resume, or graduate or professional school application. You can upload your revised work at the Submission Manager site for *Binghamton Writes*, located at http://binghamton.edu/writing/binghamtonwrites/. There, you'll be asked to create an account using your binghamton.edu email address and submit your work, along with your contact information and the name of your Writing 111 instructor.

Good luck and happy writing!

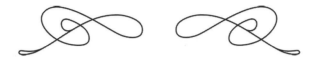

PERSONAL
ESSAYS

Julia Gladstein

Julia hails from Stony Brook, New York, and is racing to figure out what to major in but she will say she's interested in English, anthropology, and geography. Taking Writing 111 made her rediscover her love for writing, which had been dormant since her high school years. She can be found drawing portraits to a carefully constructed Spotify playlist in her spare time.

Choosing a subject for the personal essay assignment turned out to be surprisingly simple for Julia and the writing of the first draft did not take her long. The hardest part, by far, was satisfying the core requirement of the assignment—showing a reflective component involving a transition from childhood to adulthood; much revision took place as her essay began as nothing more than a collection of sporadic thoughts. The final version came through going to her professor's office hours and taking all suggestions given, mostly involving following a more cohesive structure and organization.

Julia strongly recommends taking advantage of the professor's office hours, as they can give you one-on-one feedback on essays that points you in the right direction. She must stress that no first draft is ready to turn in! Getting feedback from both peers and the professor is the real key to making a rough draft come to fruition and to making the piece an effective one. Julia also recommends writing about topics of the writer's own interest, as this is encouraged in Writing 111 and makes the process infinitely easier.

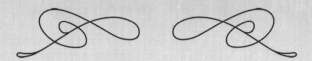

OLD SOUL

Julia Gladstein

Professor Angie Pelekidis

One weekend when I was about fifteen or sixteen, my parents and I decided to visit the Museum of Natural History. My father had grown up in Brooklyn, attending high school in Manhattan and college in the Bronx. However, after his move to the suburbs in the late 1950s he rarely paid a visit to the New York City area. Now in the midst of his seventh decade of life, the three of us opted to take the subway from Penn Station to the museum instead of walking, the intention being to save the strength in my father's arthritic knees. After boarding the crowded train car, I found a seat for him, which he gratefully seized. As the doors closed and we began to move, I watched in horror as my father plunged out of his seat and onto the floor, landing on his fragile knees and startling the young woman sitting just to his right. Other passengers stared. Now more accustomed to the car culture of Long Island than to the mass transit of the five boroughs, my father had completely forgotten about the jolt that propels subway trains forward and which native New Yorkers come to expect.

My father was officially classified as a senior citizen—sixty-five or older—when I was just six years old, a distinction my mother will come to share in three more years. This rare circumstance of age disparity between my parents and I served as the vertebrae of my home life. The minute I stepped through the front door every day, I entered a world virtually opposite to that of my peers at school. Retired from his psychiatric practice since before I began kindergarten, my father would be reading one of his leftist magazines or watching a political commentary program in the large, blue armchair that dominated the landscape of the living room. From his potbelly, to his stooped shoulders, hidden by his reclining position, to his neck straining down towards the printed page clasped in his hands, to his bloodshot eyes, he truly exemplified sluggishness. Periodically, an earth-shattering sneeze or an endless yawn would escape from his otherwise unflinching, concentrated face. My mother, radiating a much more youthful glow, would be bustling around the kitchen, in the midst of assembling an unnecessarily elaborate dinner of Olympic chicken and a massive salad, simultaneously listening to *The Oprah Winfrey Show*, *General Hospital*, or *Dr. Oz*. Since neither of my parents was employed throughout the majority of my childhood, both of them were always home to greet me and to ask how school had been, day after day, year after year, which—as I got older—became the last thing I wanted. I needed space.

As a kid having to grow up immersed in the slow lifestyle of my parents, there were many instances when I felt I was missing out on things my friends received. In terms of music, my childhood was defined by hearing a CD, usually the infamous *Beatles 1*, broadcasting through our house by means of a bulky stereo and its accompanying speakers. Once the iPod became main-stream for grade school students to own, although I secretly yearned for one, I never actually asked my parents until my freshman year of high school because I had once absentmindedly agreed with them that owning an iPod wasn't necessary. Over the course of my younger years, I tended to agree with their nonconformist way of life, thinking it was interesting, refreshing, and just cool. But more modern technology like the iPod enticed me. I started telling myself that with certain things, like a music player, there is absolutely nothing wrong with conformity.

Being thrust by default into a lifestyle that ran at a much slower pace than anything my friends knew successfully molded me, to a certain extent, into a miniature adult. What constitutes a typical Friday night for a young teenag-er? Certainly not an evening sampling exotic vegetable kormas at the newest Indian restaurant in town and listening to your parents discuss their take on the eatery's raving Zagat review in the latest *New York Times*. Certainly not heading over to see an obscure modern dance troupe while sitting transfixed in a red velvet chair for two hours. Yet this is what constitutes a typical Friday night when your mother and father are significantly, uncommonly, older than most.

Constant exposure to the kinds of things my elderly parents held dear and were relevant to their existence had me learning everything from the odd names of various prescription medications to the comedic personalities of Woody Allen and Bill Maher. I wasn't used to riding a bike alongside my father but rather to watching *World News with Peter Jennings* by his side as we ate wonderful steak dinners that have since become too tough for his few teeth to handle. I wasn't used to trailing behind my parents as we took tours of various scenic areas or traversed art museums, but to them trailing behind my fresh, energetic pace. Eventually this morphed into the opposite scenario as I got older and became painfully uninterested in what my parents considered to be a fun and exciting afternoon.

As the years went by, I began to take note of certain clues that hinted at how my parents' ages made my life and perspectives different from those of my friends and peers. When teachers in my junior high and high school classes would attempt to open students' eyes to elements of the distant past they would otherwise be oblivious to, often using the potentially enlightening opener, "You guys are probably too young to know what this was," I found myself consistently being an exception to their claims. I knew about life without caller ID and cell phones and GPS and high-definition flat-screen television sets because my parents never made use of such modern technological advancements. In history classes, discussions of the Great Depression and World War II would prompt teachers to urge us students to ask our grandparents or great grandparents about what it had been like to live during those times; I only needed to ask my father, who could be found reclining in his large, blue armchair when I returned home that day.

On the shelves in our living room stand a couple faded brown-and-white photographs of my father as a baby on the streets of Depression-era Brooklyn. By the time I first discovered them peeking out from behind bigger and brighter photographs of myself, I realized with astonishment that they possessed the same vintage aura as the ones within the pages of my history textbook. It was no wonder my father was often mistaken for my grandfather throughout my childhood. I had originally deemed those assumptions to be crazy, but now, with the help of my eighth- and eleventh-grade American history classes, I'm able to see this strange situation more realistically.

There were times when I felt wary, even ashamed, of the age peculiarity surrounding my parents. My father being mistaken for my grandfather in public was no longer amusing—it was embarrassing and freakish. Why couldn't either of them keep up with my pace, and what in the world was so difficult about using a computer? Questions like these soon resolved themselves as I myself aged, though the childish confusion was just replaced by annoyance and a constant feeling of being fed-up; I was anything but honored to serve as the built-in Windows 7 tutor for all my parents' email-deleting and image-uploading needs. Upon entering high school, it dawned on me that it was likely that some people went around wondering if I was adopted.

It became a sort of personal goal of mine throughout junior high and high school to try to hide the unorthodox ages of my parents from as many people as possible, with the exception of my closest friends. I was under the impression that this family quirk was like that one huge zit that pops up out of nowhere, beyond one's control, quickly becoming a top priority to conceal. Perceptions like this, as we all sooner or later come to understand, are highly egocentric and what may seem like a big deal or a defining trait is in fact extremely trivial in the eyes of anyone else. So now, when talking with others about what shows my family likes to watch together, instead of reluctantly saying, "You've probably never heard of it, it's this old British comedy from the 1970s my parents think is hilarious…" I can confidently offer, "It's called *Are You Being Served?* and it *is* hilarious, and how have you *not* heard of it?! Start watching it!"

No longer do I try my best to suppress information concerning my parents' ages. While I usually don't volunteer it, I willingly give it when and where it is due. After all, choosing not to dwell on things that may make you feel uneasy lifts an enormous weight off your shoulders, as it has with me, and embracing a full acceptance of such things makes life even easier. I have stopped trying to change the outdated habits of my parents that are direct results of their ages. I've realized that they're destined for a slow-paced life that drastically strays from what one would call typical of the twenty-first century. What I can control is how much I straddle embracing aspects of their lifestyle and the modern one that constantly surrounds me. Still, regardless of how far I stray from my mother and father, whether I choose T. Rex and A Tribe Called Quest over the James Taylor and Joni Mitchell they surrounded me with, I still owe them infinitely for shaping some of my most deep-seated attributes. For no matter how I look at it, my father is the person who instilled my intrinsic love of books and my tendency to read a novel on a Friday night; my father, whose home has always been his large, blue armchair, where most nights he is doing just that.

Michael Kotowski

Michael Kotowski is a junior from Merrick, New York, and is a brother of the Pi Kappa Alpha Fraternity. He is a major in both Philosophy, Politics and Law and History with a minor in Judaic Studies.

Michael works in the summer at a Jewish sleepaway camp, which he also attended as a camper from the age of 12. For this particular piece, Michael at first intended to tread upon the already much-trodden ground of a first experience as a counselor at his camp. However, when a friend asked him to describe his trip to Israel, he realized how formative a moment the trip had been in his life. Once he had settled on this topic, the first draft flowed easily from keys to screen. However, the process of editing proved to be an experience that, like his trip to Israel, forced him into the drudging realities of adulthood. The piece went through at least six different versions before Michael settled on the final one that can be read on the following pages. Like the trip to Israel, at the end of the revision process Michael felt it had been a rewarding journey. The true change to adulthood is when a person goes from being a closed, self-centered person, only interested in the mundane occurrences that affect one's own daily life, to a fully cognizant member of broader society who is conscientious of the broader world. For Michael, this adulthood began in Israel and the journey to have it fully realized will continue until he is old and gray.

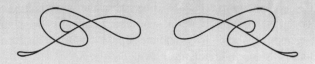

FINDING SKEPTICISM IN A HOLY PLACE

Michael Kotowski

Professor Angie Pelekidis

As I neared the *Kotel*, my steps slowed and I began to feel a peculiar sense of serenity. Regardless of what the world around me did or said, at that particular moment in time all was right. I was now close enough to touch it. I reached out a hand, then my middle finger, then my ring and index fingers, and slowly but surely my entire right hand was on the wall. I had finally arrived at the place that I had been told all Jews were meant to visit. I drew my face to the wall and lightly kissed it.

Suddenly, I began to weep uncontrollably. I wasn't sure why I was crying at first and there was a part of me that wondered if my friends would think it odd. But soon the rhythm of my tears began to draw me into an almost meditative state. I began to pray. I said the *shma*, the *vhavta*, the *shecheheyanu* and all the other prayers I could remember through a seemingly never-ending waterfall of tears. As I prayed for my mother, for my father, and for all of the people I held dear stateside, I began to think of the security booth, the wall that divides the city I was in, and then the wall that divides the people at this site, the shouting orthodox men standing at their booth with *tefillin* (boxes containing prayers that are attached to leather straps), the origin of Israeli statehood; I thought about everything that had taken place prior to me having this moment.

I cannot describe the excitement I felt being in the place that I had thought about since I was an eight-year-old boy just starting Hebrew School. I remember the first time I heard about the Western Wall, also known as the *Kotel*, in class. It was Israel day in Hebrew School, the one day every year that we devoted to learning about the ancestral homeland of the Jewish people. I remember learning about our people's ancient connection to the land from a skit that some of the teachers put on and laughing at how silly they looked dressed up in turbans and beards while pretending to be Moses and the Israelites reaching the Promised Land. I remember watching videos and talking about all the holidays and the popular culture of the modern state of Israel and all the important sites, including the *Kotel*. The teachers even built a miniature version of the *Kotel* in our dingy basement lunchroom, and in spite of the musty yellow light I could feel the replicated holiness when I was in the presence of the wall made of brown styrofoam. The last thing we learned about that day was the military history of the country. After all, Israel had already developed a rich military history in only sixty years of existence. I learned about all the many enemies of Israel, its many surrounding Arab neighbors. To me there was no distinction between Egyptians, Syrians or Palestinians; they were all just more Arabs who sought to destroy Israel.

Learning about the Israel Defense Forces and the many brave people who fought to keep Israel alive over the decades made me so proud to be Jewish. When I decided to attend a Jewish sleepaway camp the summer before sixth grade, the Zionist education that I received in Hebrew School extended into my time at camp. I made many of my best friends there, and the summer after our last year as campers we all went to Israel together. This trip would be the climax of my religious education, my friendship with my camp friends, and my personal spiritual journey through adolescence.

The day we went to the *Kotel* I felt like I was coming full circle from Israel Day in Hebrew School—there was nothing on that trip that I had been more excited to see. It was a typical Israeli summer day: completely cloudless with the sun beating down relentlessly on everything that wasn't able to find shelter under a bit of shade. Normally, I would do everything amongst a cluster of friends during that trip because, after all, this was my chance to spend time with these friends whom I had spent every summer with since I was eleven; however, that day, given the occasion, I felt it best to experience the *Kotel* on my own.

After a typically delicious lunch of *shwarma* with my friends in the old quarter of the city, our group met and proceeded to ascend the stairs to the site that was holier than any other in Judaism. The first thing I noticed about the area surrounding the wall was the security; the enclosure is entirely walled in. In order to get into the actual *Kotel* plaza, one has to go through a security depot. This area resembled a security checkpoint at an airport; I took off my shoes, placed my bag on a conveyer belt, and walked through an X-ray scanner. As I felt the hard stone ground beneath my socks and the quiet buzz of the X-ray machine, I had the sense of being in an airport terminal, about to be transported to a place I had thus far only dreamed about. I collected my bag from the conveyer belt, put my shoes back on, and stepped out into the bright plaza.

Then, I encountered the immediate division of the sexes. Women immediately turn to the right, while men proceed ahead. In accordance with Orthodox Judaism, while praying at the *Kotel*, or anywhere else for that matter, the genders must be separate. I began thinking of the United States until the Civil Rights Movement, how separate creates a situation that is the opposite of equal, with one side inevitably receiving sub-par treatment. As I looked to see where I would find a spot next to the wall amongst the men, I was relieved to find there was ample space. In fact, I could probably have gone up to the wall and had several feet on either side of me. Then I turned my head and saw the small corner of the wall that all of my female friends were crowded into to perform one of the most important things a person can do in our religion: completing a pilgrimage to this last vestige of the Ancient Temple. While all I would have to do was get a *tallis* and a *yalmuka* (a prayer shawl and cap) and proceed to the wall, all of the girls would have to squeeze into the mob of women. Slightly taken aback by this, I nonetheless eagerly proceeded toward the men's section of the *Kotel*.

Then I came to the Orthodox men, who, like the sirens in the Odyssey, were putting forth their alluring call to those passing by. As I headed toward the monolithic wall, I could hear the loud voices of these men, seeking to get all the men they could to wrap *tefillin* while they were at the wall. Although I ordinarily have no problem respecting the ways other people like to pray, these men seemed pushy and the words they used to convince pilgrims to wrap *tefillin* suggested they would be desecrating the religion and the site if they were to go to the wall without *tefillin*. While most of my friends gave in to these religious sirens, I marched ahead toward the wall. At first it seemed perfect in its pristine tan, monolithic majesty. However, as I drew nearer, I saw that the stones were jagged and imperfect. I also could make out the famous cracks between the enormous ancient works of masonry. Between these cracks are stuffed thousands of notes, some containing prayers, some containing wishes, others containing confessions, left by the many people who have visited the site.

Once I was at the wall, all I could think about was the elation I felt having finally fulfilled my religious destiny. However, the heavy security around the holy site made me slightly dismayed; it was a constant reminder that in spite of the peace and sense of oneness that I felt while I was on my pilgrimage, the country around me was in a perpetual state of alert defensiveness, terrified and ready for the very real prospect of war breaking out at any moment.

I thought about the division of the genders, which reminded me that my religion isn't perfect, that some of its practices are discriminatory and archaic. I also thought about the men who had just told me that I was doing my religion wrong at the moment when I felt I was about to do one of the most important things a Jewish person can do.

Roughly a week before this, we had visited an Arab-Israeli village of Muslim people who considered themselves Israeli. They had fought every war on the side of Israel, never siding with Palestine or any other nation in the many wars that had been fought over the land since 1948. We spoke with a woman from the village who told us that, despite the fact that they had always sided with Israel and wanted nothing more than to be full Israeli citizens, their religion made them second-class citizens. She spoke to us about how their village was omitted from many of the government benefits received by Jewish towns. How every time they traveled outside of their village they were looked upon with suspicion and treated with a lack of trust. How their government seemed to behave in a manner that indicated that they wanted nothing more than to see them pack up and leave.

Thinking back to this moment made me look with new, clear eyes at the state that was the product of my religion. Since I was eight, I had been told about the majesty and incredible feats that Jewish people had accomplished in Israel. Now I was finally there and, although I felt at home, I could no longer ignore the realities of the Jewish home state. Though the economic and military achievements of the state made me proud of my people, the open discrimination against its citizens, Jewish and non-Jewish alike, forced me to accept the fact that Israel was far from perfect. Thus far in my life I had lived with undying, unshaken faith in the Jewish religion and the Jewish people. In fact, I carried this faithfulness over to many other aspects of life and my faith in the things I valued had never truly been challenged. My visit to the *Kotel* woke me up and forced me to accept one of life's coldest, most disappointing realities. Nothing in life is perfect; everything is somehow flawed. Regardless of how much faith you put in something, if you look at it with open eyes, closely enough and for long enough, eventually you will see its imperfections, just like the imperfections in the wall. At the *Kotel* I learned that faith isn't something that should come easily and shouldn't remain unchallenged. Rather, faith should constantly be challenged in order to ensure that it isn't merely a blind acceptance of something that must be changed. I came to Israel expecting to have my undying faith and belief in my religion reaffirmed and made stronger than ever, but I left a skeptic who perpetually challenges the unquestioned imperfections that people accept at face value day in and day out.

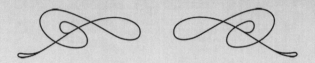

Anita Raychawdhuri

Anita Raychawdhuri is from Vestal, New York. She is an English major, with particular interests in Tolkien, Feminism and the Romantics. She is a writer for the opinion section of *Pipe Dream*, Binghamton's student newspaper. She loves yoga and reading. She hopes to one day write something that will influence someone else as she has been influenced by her favorite authors. She wants to write something with meaning.

For Anita, writing is a never-ending but nevertheless a rewarding process. There is nothing more powerful than words, and we all have a story to tell that somebody wants to hear. As an English major, writing an essay did not seem like a daunting task. However, having to write a personal essay was very new and a lot more difficult than expected. Baring your soul on paper is difficult but empowering simultaneously. Her Writing 111 instructor was Ryan Mead. Writing 111 was frustrating but rewarding. It taught her how to examine her writing under the microscope and understand her voice a lot better. As someone who'd come into the class arrogant, she learned a lot about herself and realized she did need to improve as a writer. Writing 111 certainly helped her achieve that and feel more confident in her style. The importance of revision and openness was made a lot clearer. Don't be stubborn. Be brave. Be daring. Anyone has the ability to write; you just need to take the time to do it.

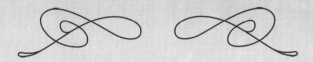

SKIN DEEP

Anita Raychawdhuri

Professor Ryan Mead

For my 19th birthday, I went out to Number 5 restaurant with my family and my boyfriend, Tom. The restaurant was so quaint and, luckily for us, my birthday fell on a Wednesday, so it wasn't too busy at all. We sat down and I ordered my favorite thing off the menu: the Greek tenderloin. It's a delicious steak (I've always loved steak) covered in a Mediterranean lemon-garlic sauce. The sauce was oily, with little bits of lemon and flakes of oregano. It smelled like it had come from a restaurant on the Aegean Coast and I savored every last bite. Then for dessert, I had a creme brûlée with a candle in it; every bite of the crunchy caramel hid an explosion of soft, creamy custard. I ate every last bit of my dinner and didn't think twice about what I was eating.

After I finished eating, I got up to go to the bathroom. I went into the stall and looked at the porcelain toilet. Seemed normal: I was going to the bathroom, nothing weird about that. But then I was in a dream; the room spun and I saw pieces of food spewing out of me and splashing across the walls of the toilet bowl like a storm. It was terrifying, but I was comforted by the fact that this was all a mirage, a painful memory of what I used to be. I am still haunted now and again, remembering how I would chew up my dinner just to regurgitate it moments later. But that night, I was stronger than that. Just two years earlier, when I had had an eating disorder, this meal would have been an ordeal, torture imposed on me by the Spanish Inquisition. Two years ago calories were my enemy; my desire to be thin was my master and I was its slave.

Near the end of my sophomore year of high school, I came home from a horrible day at school with everything falling apart. Mum called me down for dinner and I was in a horrendous mood because of a bad grade on a test I had studied for all week and a fight with my friend. I had a cheeseburger: ketchup, mayo, fries with extra salt and that cookie cake that Mum had brought home as a treat. I went to the pantry after and crammed chocolate into my mouth, round chocolate counters melting over my tongue and crushed by my teeth. Then I grabbed handfuls of chips. Barbecue? Or were they sour cream and onion? Regardless, each greasy chip was a wobbly thigh, a stomach like jelly and a flabby, cellulite butt. I ran upstairs to the bathroom, after excusing myself and thanking my Mum for dinner. I lifted up the toilet seat and shoved my fingers down my mouth. I retched a little bit and my stomach convulsed as I kept stroking the back of my throat, coaxing out the horrific calories. Kate Moss once said, "Nothing tastes as good as skinny feels," but I just couldn't make myself like mushy, green lettuce. I started to cry as the horrible mix of bile and burger shot up my trachea and plopped into the toilet. I had the bathroom fan on. Nobody could know about my shame even though I wore it on my waistline; I was ashamed of how I looked. I wanted to be beautiful and I wasn't sure how else to do it. Power came to me that day when I first decided to claw at the inside of my throat. It was exhilarating to bring my body to its knees.

I ran upstairs after that episode, filled with self-loathing, and threw myself onto my bed. I looked up with blurry eyes, scanning the room out of habit. There was a corsage on my dresser, left over from a school dance. It had a rose on it, a red rose just like the one from *Beauty and the Beast*. I remember the first time I watched that movie, I must have been about three or four, and I thought Belle was absolutely beautiful. She had a tiny waist, waif-like arms and legs, dainty little hands and feet, and big, dark eyes. One of my favorite scenes in the movie is when Belle is walking through the town and everyone is looking at her as she strolls past, saying how beautiful she is. Imagine being admired like that. I understood that the thin, small princesses were beautiful, and I wanted to be like them. Being beautiful equated to being liked. Beautiful meant validation. Princesses taught me that. I wanted Ariel's toned stomach, Jasmine's tiny waist, Snow White's slim arms and Cinderella's thin legs. I saw those girls and just knew I didn't look like them. My mother constantly told me that I was beautiful, but I never believed it. Even as a seven-year-old I was concerned about my weight. I remember one day in elementary school, sitting on the grass in gym looking down at the pasty legs coming out of my regulation gym shorts. The teacher was explaining to us the rules of some silly game and I watched the fat on my thighs swing back and forth as I moved my legs, back and forth like a pendulum, hideous matter rippling in the wind. I would never be sung about for my beauty; maybe that was why nobody really noticed me. I was invisible. I was fat, or at least I thought I was.

Next to my corsage was a stack of magazines. I bought *Teen Vogue* every month because it felt like the right thing to do as a teenage girl. The glossy pages smelled like Paris. Ads like "Cherie Dior" with a beautiful gap-toothed model holding a pink bottle in her bony hands, "GUESS Jeans" with a buxom brunette with a minuscule waist. I had moved on to some new princesses: fashion models and celebrities. I liked the fashion shoots: all tall, thin, glamorous girls in beautiful, skimpy outfits that would stretch across my skin, exposing me as if the clothes were taunting me. I liked the tips for shopping and dieting, which I tried so hard to follow. Teen Vogue tried to convince me to give up cookies and nachos and trade it in for a body to die for. The problem was I just could not, no matter how hard I tried. I thought that maybe I should recycle those magazines because they weren't going to teach me anything I didn't already know. Fat equals ugly, worthless, boring. Skinny equals pretty, nice, important.

For those two years I used food to cover up the issues I had with myself. I wanted control over something tangible, and what's more tangible than your own body? I saw a beastly thing when I looked in the mirror, a worthless and ugly creature who deserved pain. I deserved to taste vomit, to taste my sins. I was the epitome of gluttony: a fat, ugly pig. I believed it more than anything. So the smell of bile that I would tickle out was like Chanel Number 5. It was my perfume and enhancement, the secret charm to make myself desirable.

It wasn't until the beginning of my senior year that I realized I needed to stop being a victim and search for a new scent. Senior year meant applying to colleges, thinking about the future, and growing up. I knew something was wrong with me because I had constant headaches, a horrible taste in my mouth, and no energy. I had the perfect opportunity now to reinvent myself. I wanted to take a chance on me: I am good enough to be sung about in the streets. What I really wanted was a chance: a chance to try to gain control over my body. Something that took me so long to realize was that I needed to love myself before anyone else could. But to do that I had to stop vomiting, because my eating disorder was the biggest thing holding me back from valuing myself. I looked at glossy college brochures of people smiling confidently. I wanted to be like them.

The first day I tried to stop was horrible. We had Thai satays for dinner, and I used to love those before I started my long-term relationship with bulimia. I ran to the bathroom and thrust up the seat, ready to explode out all that hateful food. My fingers were creeping up to my mouth when I looked up into the mirror hanging above the sink next to the toilet. No, I told myself. This is not who you are anymore. And I walked away, my fingers shaking and peeling my fingernails.

I started slowly, trying to take my mind off food by throwing myself into other activities. I tried to think of food in a healthier way. Instead of turning to food when I had a problem, I would talk to my family or friends about it or pour my emotions into more productive activities. I needed to learn that people were willing to listen and I didn't need to hide from my feelings in my meals. It took time and I didn't immediately and perfectly get over my body issues. But small steps were still steps and progress happened, culminating in my eventual healthy and current state. Now I eat when I want with the aim of being healthy, I moderate my eating, and I don't make myself sick if I have McDonalds one day. I have enough energy now to exercise or put effort into my life, and the past few years have been brighter. I have realized that my outward appearance is worth so much less than how I think or how I act. It took me time and years of harming myself to feel ok about who I am. I understand now that I am good enough.

I looked in the mirror in my room after coming back from Number 5 Restaurant on that crisp January night. Tom went to the bathroom and I was alone in my lilac bedroom. I saw a powerful woman: someone who is strong, intelligent, opinionated, and kind. I have realized that I can't define beauty by physical attributes. Beauty as defined by the media is absolutely unattainable. I don't need to be that. I smiled at myself in the mirror, a newfound confidence that I had slowly cultivated in the last year until it reached its peak now, on my 19th birthday. I felt like a glorious, ruby phoenix risen from the ashes. I felt proud of myself and my body, more comfortable than I had in years. My past struggles are a part of me. They are weapons and armor that have allowed me to become the woman I am now. In some ways I am better equipped to handle myself and the future after struggling through loving myself. I appreciate the struggles of others more; I have a better sense of how one should value one's self and others. Being truly beautiful comes from having lovely thoughts and feelings, not your dress size. I know now that beauty is not only skin deep.

Amanda Samuels

Amanda Samuels is from Albany, New York, and she is majoring in Anthropology and minoring in Spanish. She loves playing volleyball and reading books in her spare time.

Amanda's essay, "The Hidden Scars," was not an easy topic about which to write. It was enjoyable to remember little pieces of her childhood, but it was also difficult to confront the issues she and her sister are currently facing. Her Writing 111 professor, Karen Moroski, persuaded all her students to write about a topic that had a deep emotional tie to their lives. This advice influenced everything about Amanda's essay, from the topic to the included scenes. Revising one's personal essay can be quite difficult and tedious, but it can also lead to a deeper understanding of one's self. Amanda discovered that through writing and revising this essay, she came to a better knowledge of herself and her relationship with her sister. It is not always easy to write about emotional topics, but when a writer feels truly connected to her story, she will create a much more honest and emotional piece. Writing 111 taught Amanda to express herself in a more open way and to write from life experience. Choosing a topic that was more difficult to write about, but one about which she felt strongly, allowed her to fashion a relatable and engaging essay.

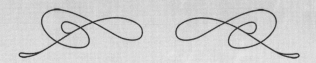

THE HIDDEN SCARS

Amanda Samuels

Professor Karen Moroski

"Come on, Amanda! Go, go, go! Don't let him pass you! Get him! Get him," my sister, Jessica, yelled. As a young child, I never realized how fortunate I was to have a normal life. I played sports, wreaked havoc on my house, and spent my days playing outdoors. Every weekend, I had soccer meets with my twin brother followed by softball games in the same park. One of my parents always drove us to matches and cheered for us, too. My sister loved to tag along. She never played sports, but she came to every one of our games that she could. She loved the excitement and energy of the kids playing ball, and her face lit up with joy when our team scored. My sister was happy because my brother and I were happy, and she just couldn't hold her glee inside. Parents of other children would slowly move away, creating an empty circle around her, because she always cheered so loudly in her shrill little voice. Their pained eardrums and slight movements in the opposite direction didn't stop my sister from reaching another octave higher the next time she let her voice loose. Rooting for the team made her feel like she was a part of our soccer club, like she belonged to something bigger than herself.

At night I would creep down from my top bunk to lie in Jessica's larger bed, and we would gossip just like normal five- and seven-year-olds do. We talked about the teachers we couldn't stand and how much candy and cake we ate at our cousin's birthday party the previous weekend. We always made it a competition to see who could gobble down the most junk food in one night. I also showed her my journals of drawings, thinking that those small pictures of dresses and suits would make me the most famous fashion designer of my day. She would pick out her favorites saying, "This is the outfit I'm going to wear when I'm teaching my first-graders." I assumed that if we both worked hard enough, we could accomplish anything. I believed in both our dreams and spent years unaware of the differences between us that would affect our lives.

In elementary school I remember walking to class holding my dad's hand and wishing that I could let go because I was a "big kid" now. I thought I was so mature and wise at the ripe old age of seven, so I was relieved when he finally let go of my hand as I reached my classroom. As my day progressed, I received assignments that I completed with my mind only half-focused on the work. Since I usually finished before the other kids, I would daydream extensively about going home and playing hide-and-go-seek around my house and backyard, though I only ever played with my brother. For reasons I didn't understand at the time, Jess had to sit at the dinner table for at least three hours most nights completing the same amount of work that took me only 30 minutes. Though she never complained, I remember seeing the longing on her face as she stared out the window at me and my brother scrambling in and out of bushes and chasing each other around the yard.

Back at school, I contemplated hiding spots like the dusty closet in the guest bedroom and the inky black space beneath my bed. The piping voice of the girl sitting at the adjoining table snapped me out of my stupor. She was looking at my chest inquisitively and asked, "What's that mark?" I looked down and realized she was pointing at my scar. Years earlier, my parents ingrained an appropriate response in my memory for how I should answer this type of question, "Oh, it's a scar. I had heart surgery when I was one-and-a-half." Her query didn't bother me or make me feel uncomfortable. I didn't know how unusual it was to have a scar running through the middle of one's chest because my sister had the exact same mark marring her skin.

When I was ten, Jessica and I became involved with the American Heart Association. We spoke at events, raised money and formed a team to participate in the annual Heart Walk. She was our team leader. She was gregarious and outgoing, which partnered perfectly with my introverted personality. In order to raise as much money we could, my sister and I walked around the neighborhood and knocked on doors asking for donations. Jess did most of the talking. Once in a while she would say, "Amanda, you really need to get over your fear of talking to strangers. It's really going to hold you back," and then she would make me ask for donations at the next house on our path. We walked up and down street after street, with me always walking on the outside since she had a tendency to stray in one direction or another if she wasn't paying attention. Ever since her surgery, Jess often forgot where her body was in relation to the rest of the world. One day after school we decided to go on a bike ride, and she almost got hit by a bus. As she was riding, she'd slowly crept toward the middle of the street until her tires were only inches away from the yellow line running down the middle of the road. We laughed about it then, but I remember the panicked look on her face when she finally looked up and realized the precarious situation she was in.

Aside from our work with the American Heart Association, we had many other annual traditions, like doctor's visits. I always enjoyed going to the cardiologist. The doctor smeared chilled goo on my chest so that he could look for any problems with my heart. I found it fascinating that I could look at what seemed to be a television show starring my internal organs. During one particular visit when I was in sixth grade, I was playing a basic spelling game with my mom and sister as we sat in the office waiting to see the doctor. I noticed that I was able to answer more of my mother's questions, and Jess began to get frustrated. I couldn't understand why she was so discouraged by the inability to spell a few words. Seeing my confusion and my sister's frustration, my mom sat us down, looked at me, and said, "Jessica has a harder time remembering things, so you learn more easily than she does." I was confused, but my sister seemed to understand what my mom said, like they had already had this exact conversation. How could I be more adept at learning? My sister knew so much more than I did about everything. I idolized her, so how was it possible that I could memorize and learn more than she could?

Slowly I began to see the lasting effects of my sister's surgeries, and the damage done to her brain. It was simple misfortune that the scalpel had nicked my sister's heart. Simple misfortune that the emergency bypass had starved her brain of oxygen. Simple misfortune, and a part of her died. She struggled with her schoolwork and didn't make friends as easily as I did, due to her lack of appropriate social skills. She couldn't walk down the road without drifting from the side because she had lost her depth perception. Years passed, and as I entered high school, our relationship began to crumble. She often had a problem with understanding tone, so she would often say hurtful or ignorant things without meaning to offend anyone. As a young child, I never understood that her cutting words were arrows piercing my skin, but I gradually noticed she spoke more cruelly to me than anyone else in our family. She treated me as if she was my superior, ordering me around like a mother disciplining her young child. My ears caught every snide comment, and I started to retaliate. I could no longer stand being the target of her hate. I turned to my mom, asking her why Jessica was much more malicious toward me than toward my brother or the rest of my family. My mom simply said, "She's jealous."

By the time I reached high school, I had surpassed my sister in almost every aspect of our lives. As a senior in high school I was already helping her with the math homework she received as a college student. I edited papers she wrote for her classes and assisted her in studying for exams. Not only had I excelled at school, I also played varsity and club volleyball, while she watched from the sidelines. Although I understood that it was her jealousy causing her to say unkind words, that couldn't diminish my anger. Every barb in her words wounded my pride and self-esteem. I didn't deserve to be treated so coldly. I refused to be her punching bag, so I hit back.

We had terrible fights, spewing malicious words and hoping they would hit as hard as a fist. I don't remember what caused half our arguments, but in the middle of one screaming match during my junior year of high school, she shouted, "You're worthless. You are less than nothing." Those words twisted a knife in my gut. I yelled back, calling her ugly names hoping to cause her the same pain, but she just shook her head and walked away. Afterwards, I replayed our fight over and over, picking apart the details. Was I really "nothing" to her? I knew we didn't have the best relationship, but I was taught that family is supposed to love each other despite their problems. I couldn't figure out where our love turned sour, and the question nagged at the back of my mind for days. I thought over her words again and finally asked myself a new question: Is that how she feels about herself?

As time passed, I couldn't stop thinking about the way Jessica viewed herself. How could I have been so blind? I knew all of this hatred and tension between us stemmed from her disabilities and my lack thereof. I could play sports, make new friends, and go to a four-year university, while all her life she knew she would never be able to do the same. I had come to hate the snide remarks she spewed with venom and the demeaning manner with which she treated me, so a small part of me came to hate her, too. How had I not seen that she also hated a part of herself? Every day she faced the demoralizing fact that no matter how much effort she put into achieving her dreams, she might never accomplish them. She would never be as smart, athletic, or successful as a typical person. She was supposed to be the older, wiser, and more accomplished child, but it was all stripped from her grasp the moment a piece of her brain died.

I am the permanent reminder of all my sister lost. I am the image of what she could have been if only the surgery had gone differently. How could she possibly love that reflection? It's a question I have pondered, but I have yet to find an answer. Perhaps the only way to know is to ask her. But I—we—are not ready yet for that conversation. For now, the question remains unanswered.

OP-EDS

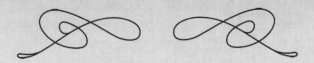

Kasey Muchnicki

Kasey Muchnicki is from East Northport, New York, and has lived there her whole life. She is a Chemistry major following the pre-dental track. Kasey is also a part of the Binghamton University Volleyball team. Playing piano and reading books are activities that she enjoys when she has free time.

Kasey found the topic of her Op-Ed, the SAT, to be quite interesting because her younger brother would be in the first class to take the revised SAT. While researching the changes, she became aware that these innovations would not benefit the next generation taking the test. For Kasey, the hardest part of writing the paper was writing the rough draft. Once her thoughts were organized on paper, the revising and editing were much easier. For revision, she completely reorganized the way the essay was structured, took out paragraphs, added new ones, and changed the essay so that it would be more comprehensible to the reader.

Writing 111 proved to be an excellent course to introduce Kasey to different genres at the college level of writing and to serve as a basis for essays to come in the future for other classes. This course helped develop her writing and so far has been one of the most beneficial classes she has taken at Binghamton University.

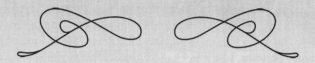

DUMBING DOWN THE SAT

Kasey Muchnicki

Professor Wendy Stewart

An·i·mad·vert [an-*uh*-mad-**vurt**]

Verb

1.   To pass criticisms or censure on; speak out against (Oxford Dictionaries)

Do you know the definition of animadvert off the top of your head? I wouldn't believe that many people do. If "animadvert" had shown up on the SAT I took, I would have never gotten the answer right. I took the PSAT twice, sat through long and tedious SAT courses, and studied and stressed for hours on end to prepare for this one test that was going to make or break my college admission. Now, nobody has to worry about obscure, lesser-known words that show up on the SAT anymore because they're being eliminated. Some may think this is the right move made by the College Board, but I have many "animadversions" regarding this new, revamped SAT.

For the second time in a decade, the College Board has decided to reshape the SAT, this time for the 2016 academic year. On the new test, the essay will no longer be mandatory, although it will be optional. Consequently, the top score will be a 1600 instead of 2400. The essay will be based on analyzing documents and providing an argument to persuade the reader. In addition, the vocabulary section will not include obscure words that students will memorize and never use again; it will be comprised of words commonly utilized in college. The math section will be narrowed down to focus on only three topics: algebra, data analysis, and introduction to advanced math. According to the College Board, "The redesigned SAT will engage students in close reading and honor the best work of the classroom" (College Board).

In my opinion, that's code for "making it easier." By making these changes to the SAT, the College Board has made the test much simpler, and only so many changes can be made until the test is no longer effective. According to Zachary Goldfarb, a policy editor at the *Washington Post*, studies have shown that the SAT favors richer, more educated families. This is a major problem because that means the SAT is not an effective way to measure students' abilities, and that it favors students of higher socioeconomic status. The College Board is teaming up with the Khan Academy to make free test-prep available to all students and to aid those who cannot afford the expensive preparation classes. The Khan Academy is a non-profit organization that provides free education to anyone across the globe (College Board). According to Sam Khan of the Khan Academy, "For too long, there's been a well-known imbalance between students who could afford test-prep courses and those who couldn't" (College Board). By making these modifications to the SAT, the College Board aims to level the playing field for lower-income students, but I believe that, in fact, these changes will not realistically alter the dynamic enough.

The College Board has elected to remove "SAT words" from the test: "'SAT words' will no longer be vocabulary students may not have heard before and are not likely to use again. Instead, the SAT will focus on words that students will use consistently in college and beyond" (College Board). Because why would the College Board want to test SAT words on the SAT? The vocabulary will now consist of words like "synthesis" and "empirical" (Lewin). By making the vocabulary simpler, students will not have to stress over studying as much for the SAT because the words will be more or less common sense. If words like "empirical" and "synthesis" are not a part of students' vocabulary already, then much more drastic measures need to be taken than just modifying the SAT.

Now, if making the reading section easier is not enough, do not fret: the math is getting simpler too. According to the College Board, "The math section will draw from fewer topics that evidence shows most contribute to student readiness for college and career training" (College Board). Let me translate that for you: The College Board is not going to test as much math content. In my opinion, if a student has taken pre-calculus in school already, the math section was a breeze. I took the PSAT twice without taking pre-calculus first, and the math section was extremely hard. After I had taken the class, my score in that section increased substantially. Obviously, students who haven't taken this class yet are at a disadvantage, but if free test-prep was available online, access to this topic would be readily available and anyone can learn it. Just narrowing down the math topics and simplifying them on the SAT isn't going to close the score gap between higher- and lower-income families. Because the Khan Academy has a mission to provide free education to anybody, they are trying to alleviate this problem by allotting free SAT preparation online to any student (College Board). This is very beneficial to students of lower socioeconomic status because they will now have equal access to information and be able to learn the same concepts that the students from richer families have. There may be a problem with this because the lowest income brackets may not have readily available access to the computer and internet. Another problem students may encounter are the schools and environment they are learning in. Some students may not be able to teach themselves subjects they have never learned previously, and some of the courses they take may not be of the same caliber as courses in other schools.

What will making the essay optional do for the SAT? It is probable that most students will elect to write it regardless, and many colleges will require that applicants take it. I do agree that this adjustment to the essay will benefit test takers; instead of writing on any topic under the sun, test takers will now have to "analyze evidence and explain how an author builds an argument to persuade an audience" (College Board). This contrasts from the current essay, where test takers can easily write about anything. I concede that this is change for the better because test takers are using skills to develop a position and argument on a topic and using facts to support it. Furthermore, people may be in favor of these modifications to the SAT because they may believe that testing less challenging subjects will help students of lower socioeconomic status, but in reality it does not help it enough. There is a much larger problem for these students that needs to be addressed.

Because the test will not be as challenging, the scores will be much higher on average than they have been in the past. Therefore, colleges will expect a score closer to perfect than they do right now. This actually contradicts what the College Board is attempting to accomplish. It will become tougher to get accepted to colleges because perfection will be expected more than ever. What is even worse is that the penalty for guessing will be eliminated. Test takers will be rewarded for simply guessing on a right answer rather than omitting the question because they did not know it. This seems counter-effective to me. In my experience, I liked the penalty for guessing because people couldn't get free points for simply guessing the right answer. If I were in the admission board's shoes, I would want the penalty for guessing to be included on the SAT. The penalty for guessing eliminates points given for lucky answers and more accurately portrays the score received. It will raise the grades even further, yet again counteracting the alterations.

An issue posed has been whether the changes made to the SAT are in fact solving the problem of benefitting more well-off students who can afford to pay for tutors and test preparation. Studies have shown that the SAT does favor richer families. By making these changes to the SAT, the College Board believes they are leveling the playing field. In an article by Zachary Goldfarb of the *Washington Post*, he collects data provided by the College Board that reveals SAT scores are highly correlated with income, parental education, ethnicity, and scores by PSAT participation. "The organization's own data show that wealthier Americans, from more educated families, tend to do far better on the test" (Goldfarb). One change that will actually benefit students is The College Board's pairing up with the Khan Academy to provide students with free test-prep. I think this a smart move made by the College Board, because these inequalities exist and everyone should have access to equal education. In addition to providing free test preparation, they are allowing four fee waivers for college applications for students who economically qualify for it. This way, these students can have access to apply for these colleges regardless of their economic standing (College Board). They should have provided free test prep a long time ago, so that people who cannot afford the expensive SAT classes can have access to the same thing wealthier families have. By allotting free test prep, these changes to the SAT would not be necessary.

These changes are not just being made to provide assistance to students that may not have as much access to test preparation, but because more students are now choosing to take the ACT rather than the SAT. It's nothing more than a business ploy. Both of these tests strive to accomplish the same goal, to provide a standardized test for colleges to base admission on, but right now the ACT is winning so the College Board must respond. According to the article "SAT to Drop Essay Requirement, But Colleges Might Still Require It" by Larry Gordon of the *LA Times*, "About 1.6 million students took the SAT last year, and more than 1.7 million took the ACT.... In some ways, the new SAT will become more like the ACT, which has an optional writing section that many colleges require. The SAT also will switch to the ACT model of grading, in which only correct answers are counted and students are not dinged for wrong ones." Maybe these changes are being made to only look like the College Board is trying to help lower-income students, but in reality it is to compete with the ACT. Students who come from lower-income families have access to libraries and other free and public means of attaining information. Also, many public schools will pay for some students to take the PSAT, so there's no issue there. And on top of that, everyone will now have access to the same test preparation because of the Khan Academy. With all these factors, there is no excuse for people to do better or worse depending on their socioeconomic status.

By making these changes to the SAT, the College Board in reality isn't doing anything to help students with a lower income: "Chucking the essay and changing some of the questions don't fix those problems" ("Re-examining the SAT"). This transformation will just make it easier for students to get higher scores, making the competition even harsher. The major beneficial change is the free test prep being provided, and so the gap between students of high and low socioeconomic status is potentially reduced a bit. Free test prep could just be added without making any of the other detrimental changes to the SAT. These modifications will subsequently not help students but harm them. The only way to level out SAT scores would be to reduce socioeconomic inequality, which will not happen by modifying the SAT. The College Board should not "dumb down" the SAT because students entering college need to think at a more advanced level.

Works Cited

"Animadvert." Definition. *Oxforddictionaries.com*. Oxford University Press, 2014. Web. 1 May 2014.

College Board, The. "The College Board Announces Bold Plans to Expand Access to Opportunity; Redesign of the SAT." *collegeboard.org*. The College Board, 19 Mar. 2014. Web. 3 May 2014.

Goldfarb, Zachary. "These Four Charts Show How the SAT Favors Rich, Educated Families." *Washington Post*. Washington Post, 5 Mar. 2014. Web. 6 Mar. 2014.

Gordon, Larry. "SAT to Drop Essay Requirement, But Colleges Might Still Require It." *Los Angeles Times*. Los Angeles Times, 5 Mar. 2014. Web. 20 Mar. 2014.

Lewin, Tamar. "A New SAT Aims to Realign With Schoolwork." *New York Times*. New York Times, 5 Mar. 2014. Web. 20 Mar. 2014.

"Re-examining the SAT is (A) Good; (B) Bad; (C) Overdue; (D) None of the Above." Editorial. *Los Angeles Times*. Los Angeles Times, 6 Mar. 2014. Web. 6 Mar. 2014.

Evan Neighley

Evan Neighley is from Mattituck, New York, a small town on the north fork of Long Island. He intends to major in Actuarial Sciences, as he has a strong interest in mathematics and economics. When he isn't playing soccer with his friends, Evan can be found supporting Arsenal FC, his favorite soccer team.

This was the first time Evan had been asked to write anything like an opposite-editorial, so while this made the process relatively challenging, it was also intriguing to him. For both the polished draft and final portfolio, Evan revised by taking every suggestion made by his classmates and professor into careful consideration. His editor, Justin Nevin, provided a great deal of help when it came to the final revision for publication.

Writing 111 contributed to this paper in particular by teaching him the importance of Rogerian rhetoric, a technique that finds common ground in a debate rather than focusing on only one side of it. With help from Wendy K. Stewart, his Writing 111 professor, Evan was able to improve the overall quality of his writing. He would like to emphasize the importance of topic choice, as it is his understanding that this is crucial to writing effectively. Evan believes that choosing a topic you are interested in will not only make writing the essay more enjoyable, but will also improve the quality of the piece.

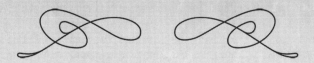

DIGITAL CURRENCY: CURRENTLY A DIGITAL DANGER

Evan Neighley

Professor Wendy Stewart

At this very moment, there exists a currency that holds more power than you could even fathom. A virtual currency that not only retains complete legality, but is also protected by a number of complex algorithms. These algorithms form a coded encryption so incredibly unique and dominant that given the opportunity, you could use this currency to purchase things you would never be able to using that paper you call your "money." I'm talking about a heavily mathematics-based creation with so much potency that, unlike the US dollar, potentially no government could touch it or keep any record of it for that matter. Moreover, it's something that's available to you with one simple purchase—or better yet, you could even make your own. That's right. *Make your own currency*, right at home. The idea may seem a bit dangerous but nonetheless intriguing, right? Now what you may not know is that the transactions involved with this creation are totally anonymous, and that with this creation comes no definitive security, no guarantee of worth, and a consistently volatile fluctuation in value as well. In addition, you may not have been aware that thousands of people are using this creation for the wrong things with little to no risk of being caught. Sounds kind of sketchy, doesn't it? In reality, it's quite a controversial concept.

This invention is known as the bitcoin. Supposedly created by an individual with the alias Satoshi Nakamoto, the world's very first potentially successful "digital currency" was initially introduced in 2009 and has since seen its ups and downs. These milestones and setbacks have ranged from spikes in popularity and booms in value to a partially tarnished reputation and crashes in worth. According to Andy Greenberg, a technology, privacy, and information-security reporter for *Forbes Magazine*, it has become an especially popular topic since the arrest of Ross Ulbricht, the alleged creator of an online website known as the *Silk Road* that used bitcoins (again, a legal type of currency) to traffic illegal goods and services, including a wide variety of drugs. As more and more companies and websites have begun to accept the bitcoin as means of purchasing things online, the bitcoin has found its way into the headlines of a number of top news organizations. What many can't seem to put their finger on is whether this invention represents a potential for strong benefits or extreme consequence and whether we should allow it to attain its full capabilities as a universal currency. While I agree that it holds a great deal of potential in terms of benefiting society, I believe that the advantages of using this digital currency don't come close to outweighing its potentially negative consequences. Therefore, as it stands now, the bitcoin is too dangerous to be put to practical use in everyday life.

Sure, right now it may seem as though the crypto-currency sounds too unreliable to even consider its implementation, but in reality, it carries many attributes that thousands of people would—or already do—benefit from. For example, using bitcoins provides privacy that is unmatched by any bank account. In his discussion concerning the privacy associated with bitcoins, accountant and expert in economic philosophy Ron Moran notes that, without revealing any personal information or credentials, an individual can make his or her own "wallet" for bitcoins on his/her computer virtually an infinite number of times over. Something like this not only grants us more anonymity than any the average bank account—as it is not monitored by another party—but also limits the access of funds to entrances that you designate yourself. Privacy is something that people like, especially fiscal privacy, which brings us to the newly introduced currency's next benefit. With all of the identity fraud and theft today, it's difficult to trust most transactions online using a credit card. *New York Times* columnist Joe Nocera claims that the bitcoin provides a way around this, making "transactions much easier while cutting down on the rampant credit card fraud and identity theft that exists online." Because of the privacy it offers, the use of the bitcoin in online transfers of funds would reduce the frequency of these types of crimes, sparing people stress and financial crises alike. Clearly, there are multiple ways the implementation of the bitcoin would benefit society in terms of privacy.

But then we must think. Privacy is something we value, considerably so with online transactions. But the bitcoin offers a ton of privacy—perhaps even *too* much. In my opinion, the bitcoin grants its users a dangerous amount of confidentiality, so much, in fact, that this currency's application is rendered impractical. For example, the aforementioned anonymity of this digital currency, combined with the bitcoin's power to purchase a wide variety of illegal things (as a result of its privacy), would open up an ocean of opportunity for those with criminal intentions. While it is known that these types of transactions already exist, using bitcoins just makes them easier, quicker, and potentially untraceable, giving criminals incentive to make illicit purchases more often. People would be able to hire hit men from a local café, and terrorists would potentially be able to purchase bombs and fully automatic weapons with the simple click of a button. The possibilities are astounding, and I'm not the only one who thinks so. According to Ron Moran, "bitcoins would be the perfect tool for unscrupulous characters like terrorists and drug smugglers who want to exchange currency anonymously with a system that is not vulnerable to government intervention." Any bitcoin user who is serious about large illegal transactions can and will take the necessary steps to ensure complete anonymity from the government and leave no trace behind. It is obvious that privacy is included with the digital coin, but that isn't necessarily as good a thing as one might initially think.

To continue with some of the pros that could come out of the practiced use of the bitcoin, it is worth noting that Satoshi Nakamoto's creation actually has a limited supply. As Ron Moran asserts, once all of the bitcoins are made available through a relatively complicated "mining" process (which anybody can take part in, so long as they have a high-powered computer and a ton of time), their production will cease. Many believe that the current global monetary system—one that revolves around conversions between many different currencies—is inefficient and needs correction. It occurs to many that, should the bitcoin be successfully put in place as a universal medium for financial transactions, there exists potential for a much more efficient system. The only problem is this currency technically isn't worth anything—literally, no face value. The only reason it is worth anything right now is because people *believe* it's worth something. In reality this is how all currency works, but the difference is there is no "bitcoin government" or higher power that recognizes value in the coin. The US dollar has value because the government says it does, and things such as precious stones are worth money because they are used for expensive jewelry. However, the bitcoin is worth something only because the *people* make it so, and therefore no government accepts it as having any value. As a result, the digital currency has consistently volatile fluctuation in value, and in fact there is no guarantee that the bitcoin will retain any of that value at all. On top of this, unlike that supplied by banks, there isn't necessarily a strong security for these coins; one could easily lose all of their coins, with no way of getting them back. There exists potential for people to lose thousands, or even millions of dollars, a potential that turned into an actuality in late February of this year, when the world's largest and most popular bitcoin exchange experienced a financial disaster. In his report on the matter, tax, finance, and business expert Cameron Keng explains how Mt. Gox experienced a hack or security breach that resulted in the loss of around $409,000,000. While this may not seem like a lot of money by to-day's standards, market and finance reporter Steven Perlberg explains that individual clients have lost anywhere from just a few hundred to hundreds of *thousands* of dollars. Many of these same individuals have claimed that their lost funds were not just investments to expand wealth, but entire retirement savings—a true crisis indeed. As one might easily see, not only was this a financial disaster for the company itself, but also for all of those who were Mt. Gox customers. This fiscal catastrophe represents a prime example of a huge risk that comes with the use of bitcoins.

But don't give up on this coin just yet, for what could possibly be its greatest benefit has yet to be mentioned. The bitcoin has a great deal of potential in terms of microfinance; it could help out small businesses all over the world. In his recent discussion of bitcoins and their influence on microfinance, science reporter Vasudevan Mukunuth explains that small businesses "need to set up complex bank transfer wires between them—the producers—and their global consumers, often through middlemen such as PayPal whose participation comes with an automatic loss of value, around 7 to 10 percent of the transaction." This is where Nakamoto's creation comes in. You see, what's special about the bitcoin is that it can evade the expenses that come with foreign exchange fees, the exact expenses that make it difficult for up-and-coming small businesses to expand and gain more popularity.

It all sounds great; however, the problem with this is that, as noted by The Bitcoin Foundation, many people are still unaware that something as powerful as the bitcoin is even in existence. While it is true that every day more and more businesses and companies are beginning to accept bitcoins as means of purchase, the coin is nowhere near popular enough to have a significant effect on small businesses (Bitcoin Foundation). Therefore, the coin would need to gain popularity, meaning more coins would have to be out there, meaning more coins will potentially be used for the wrong things. Is it really worth it?

To reiterate, while I concede that the implementation of the bitcoin presents a variety of benefits to society, I still maintain that they are far too unstable and unregulated to represent any practical usage without setbacks. An individual might object that there are ways to prevent the potentially negative outcomes of accepting bitcoins like other currencies, to which I would reply that the mathematical encryptions and algorithms along with the total anonymity of the bitcoin makes it practically untouchable. With the bitcoin's quickly growing popularity, it's an important topic for discussion. Therefore, in my opinion it's evident that a serious amount of strict regulations would need to be put in place before this currency could be used in everyday life.

Works Cited

Bitcoin Foundation, The. "Frequently Asked Questions." *Bitcoinfoundation. org*. 2012. Web. 21 Mar. 2014

Greenberg, Andy. "Alleged Silk Road Creator Ross Ulbricht Hit With 'Kingpin' Charge, Another 20 Years Minimum Prison Time." *Forbes Magazine*. Forbes Magazine, 4 Feb. 2014. Web. 16 Mar. 2014.

Keng, Cameron. "Bitcoin's Mt. Gox Goes Offline, Loses $409M—Recovery Steps and Taking Your Tax Losses." *Forbes Magazine*. Forbes Magazine, 25 Feb. 2014. Web. 1 May 2014.

Moran, Ron. "Pros and Cons of Using Bitcoins." *Frontiers.com*, 22 Nov. 2013. Web. 6 Mar. 2014.

Mukunuth, Vasudevan. "Bitcoins: Missing the Real Revolution." *The Hindu*. The Hindu, 6 Jan. 2014. Web. 21 Mar. 2014.

Nocera, Joe. "The Bitcoin Blasphemy." *New York Times*. New York Times, 28 Feb. 2014. Web. 7 Mar. 2014.

Perlberg, Steven. "The Statements From People Who Lost Their Money On Mt. Gox Are Seriously Sad." *Business Insider*. Business Insider, 4 Mar. 2014. Web. 22 Oct 2014.

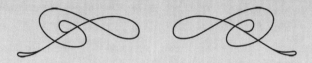

Tyler Rock

Tyler Rock is from Brooklyn, New York, and is currently majoring in Psychology with hopes of becoming a children's therapist. Outside of academics, Tyler enjoys playing the clarinet and has been doing so for the past eight years. His love of playing and listening to music helped inspire him to get his first tattoo around his arm. With writing being one of his favorite things to do, Writing 111 was the perfect class for him.

Tyler wrote his op-ed on the Common Core curriculum, which happens to be very relevant to New York City at the moment and has a huge impact on most of the country. His original plans were to become a high school teacher because of how important he knows education is for generations to come. Even though the Common Core never personally affected Tyler, his passion for education motivated him to write his essay. Having this motivation made writing the op-ed a lot easier and the Writing 111 process a lot smoother.

Writing 111 resulted in the best pieces Tyler has ever written. The best advice he has to offer for this class is to pick topics near and dear to you. Writing about something you are passionate about helps put a part of you in your essay. Tyler's instructor, Jason Allen, also helped him realize that with simple revisions and by rewording sentences, you can make your essay sound a lot better. If you put full effort into your writing and make it your own, you will have amazing results to be proud of.

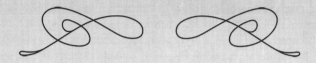

ROTTEN TO THE CORE

Tyler Rock

Professor Jason Allen

Karen Lamoreaux shared a fourth grade Common Core math problem in front of the Arkansas Board of Education and explained how the Common Core standards expect students to follow "108 steps to solve the problem" (Stossel). The example she used was: "Mr. Yamato's class has 18 students. If the class counts around by a number and ends with 90, what number did they count by?" Most people would respond by saying that they divided 90 by 18 and reached the answer of five. Although this outcome is correct, if you were taking the Common Core examination you would be marked incorrect because you didn't follow the 108 steps. This question is just a small taste of how the Common Core over-determines the idea of standardization without considering the differences amongst students as individuals.

The Common Core is, according to its website, "a set of high-quality academic standards in mathematics and English language arts/literacy" ("About the Standards"). The Common Core has six standards, and summed up their goals are to get students to think critically based on rigorous content to prepare them for college and the global economy and society. Currently forty-five states, the District of Columbia, four territories, and the Department of Defense Education Activity have adopted this Common Core curriculum (Common Core Website). As an alumnus of New York City elementary, middle, and high schools, I can attest to the fact that the education system is already far from perfect, and something that sounds as immaculate as the Common Core's goals is bound to have a plethora of flaws if you dig deeper within.

The Common Core tries to challenge students and strengthen their critical thinking skills, which can be very beneficial; however, the way they are executing this is not working. To start at the kindergarten level with a curriculum that is part of a long-term plan to prepare students for college makes no sense at all. Who in their right mind should be worrying about college for a kindergarten student? Things that use to be taught to second graders in the old curriculum are now being taught to kindergarteners in the new curriculum (Meador). From learning simple concepts like addition and the ABC's, they would also need to be more analytical and detailed. While I am all for critical thinking, the cost at such a young age is the socialization skills that these children need. Many younger students will grow to hate going to school because of how demanding and difficult it is so early on. We are dealing with the early development of human beings, not programming robots. This machine-like idea begins to shape the creation of standardization.

When dealing with something as fragile as children's education, one who creates the curriculum should have a first-hand experience with early development. Unfortunately, the Common Core's mechanical plan was drafted by the wrong people. Instead of having input from classroom teachers between grades K–3, early childhood professionals, and parents, the Common Core was made up by members of College Board, publishers of the ACT, and some associated with Achieve. Feedback groups were mostly university professors, and it was later revealed that throughout this whole process, only one classroom teacher was involved (Karp). It is obvious that for drafting a "college ready" curriculum you would need college professors and the College Board involved; however, you also need a fair number of grade school teachers because they have the most relevant expertise and will be the ones implementing this project. This curriculum diminishes the idea of people thinking for themselves and critically—what the Common Core entails—by forcing teachers to execute a curriculum they had no input in. The Common Core created puppets of teachers, which subsequently is creating puppets of students. With puppet students, our future leaders will have little diversity on how they think because of the current leaders treating us like pawns.

The standardization that the Common Core is creating begins to hurt the students and their unique ways of learning. To start, there is no equivalency exam for students with special needs, which will not only hurt the students with special needs but also the school overall (Meador). Even though it is said by the Common Core website that it is up to the teachers to adapt to their students as they normally would, that's a very difficult task to achieve when preparing for these Common Core examinations. Every year, teachers have to adapt to new students, which is challenging enough for them, but now the students need to adapt from how they used to learn to the "Common Core way." There is too drastic a change in a short period of time for results to happen immediately. Because these exams have a big impact deciding whether students get promoted to the next grade or which middle/high school they attend, the continuous failing from Common Core exams cannot keep occurring. Since we cannot avoid testing, the curriculum should give students and teachers more time to adapt, or not make learning a tedious, one-way process. Whether you have special needs or not, every student should be viewed as an individual because each and every person learns in his or her own way.

My sister took the first Common Core incorporated state exams in 2013 when she was in the seventh grade. A very intelligent girl who's especially proficient in math, she earned 4s (the highest you can receive) on all of her state exams in previous years, but then received a 2 (which doesn't meet the proficiency standards) during the one year that actually mattered. In New York City, seventh grade is the year high schools look at when deciding whom they want in their schools, and she did not get into the high school of her choice—most likely because of this test score. She was absolutely devastated and her self-esteem was definitely hurt. This curriculum can't measure a student's intelligence and aptitude when it's not being implemented properly within the state. The Common Core's idea of implementation was changing gears mid-race, which resulted in a poor performance in not only my sister's exams but also the majority of students throughout New York City.

Students are being "prepared for the real world" ineffectively when the emphasis is on examinations. Studies have shown that standardized tests are fairly good indicators of a student's knowledge, but this doesn't mean a curriculum should be designed solely for an examination. Personally, I do better on exams when I am taught the material and actually take something from the class compared to what the Common Core does, which is prepare you for the exams themselves. Although standardized exams are a necessary evil, to face it we shouldn't standardize the students and methods of learning. The Common Core curriculum should only serve as a blueprint that students overtime should fill in themselves.

The Common Core emphasizes how their standards will prepare students for the real world and college. How is requiring students to do 108 steps to solve a simple one-step math problem relevant in today's society? Doing things quickly and efficiently gets you further in today's society, not doing the tedious process of 108 steps. What the Common Core should do, however, is teach a variety ways of solving the problems because the more ways you know how to do something, the more versatile you will be. By standardizing students to solve a problem in one way and one way only, you lose sight of the goal of the Common Core, which is critical thinking.

By standardizing a whole student body, the lack of money becomes an even bigger issue. The Common Core's master plan, as expected, doesn't come free of charge. Schools that aren't as well-funded as others will have a lot of trouble keeping up with the Common Core because it requires new technology to take the Common Core Standards Assessments. Also, many new textbooks will be required, which many schools cannot afford. Many schools will have trouble even getting the materials to help teach this Common Core curriculum (Meador). What the Common Core failed to realize is that money has a significant impact in today's society on how one gets an education. The Common Core needs to stop assuming all students are identical because it puts everyone on the same playing field, but based on a school's budget, every school is already on a different one.

If the Common Core were to be implemented properly in New York, there would most likely be a lot less controversy. In the 2009–2010 school year, New York State adopted the Common Core standards, and by the 2012–2013 school year the Common Core was integrated within the state tests of grades 3–8 (NYC DOE Website). This lack of preparation time is shown through the results of the first state tests incorporating the Common Core standards. In 2013, 31 percent of students in New York met or exceeded the proficiency standard in language arts in comparison to the year prior when 55 percent scored as well ("New York's Common Core Test Scores"). This shows a much higher rating for proficiency prior to incorporation of the Common Core standards. Many suggest that you can't compare the two exams because they contain very different content, but you can't ignore statistics like these either. Obviously, the results demonstrate how difficult the new state exams were and how poorly students and teachers were prepared for them. I do believe the Common Core has a lot of potential and a good intention, but the way it has been implemented thus far has not been successful, as seen by the statistics.

The Common Core is intended to prepare students for college and the real world, but their idea of standardization is hurting schools, teachers, and students themselves in the progress. Schools are losing money while being forced to ultimately fail students who can't adapt to the Common Core. For the Common Core to be as effective as possible, they should start fresh with incoming kindergarten students and reevaluate the standards for each grade. As of right now, it appears fairly unreasonable to just throw second grade material at kindergarteners as well as changing gears on students who are used to the old curriculum. Also, what needs to be recognized is that students need a path to be guided down while letting them pave the way for themselves. One cannot be successful in the "real world" and "college" when forced to follow a standard. When you want a new ripe apple, you don't use the core to replant it: you only need the seeds from the core to result in a flourishing apple tree. The execution of the Common Core should be thrown out like the core of an apple, when the goals of the curriculum are the only way to successfully reproduce flourishing and unique students for our future.

Works Cited

"About the Standards." *Corestandards.org*. Common Core State Standards Initative, n.d. Web. 23 Mar. 2014.

Karp, Stan. "The Problems with the Common Core." *Rethinkingschools.org*. N.p. 20 Sept. 2013. Web. 23 Mar. 2014.

Meador, Derrick. "What Are Some Pros and Cons of the Common Core Standards?" *About.com*. Web. 23 Mar. 2014.

"New York's Common Core Test Scores." Editorial. *New York Times*. New York Times, 7 Aug. 2013. Web. 24 Mar. 2014.

NYC Department of Education Website. "NYC and the Common Core." *Schools.nyc.gov.*, n.d. Web. 24 Mar. 2014.

Stossel, John. "Common Core." *townhall.com*. Salem Communications, 1 Jan. 2014. Web. 24 Mar. 2014.

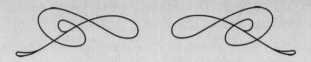

Rachel Willison

Rachel is a Mathematics major and Computer Science minor from Annapolis, Maryland. In high school, Rachel ran track and field, was secretary of the French Honor Society, and sailed on her school's varsity sailing team. She now spends her free time rowing on Binghamton's varsity crew team and running through the Nature Preserve.

As a student in Writing 111, Rachel has expanded her literary abilities beyond what she hoped to achieve. While writing is not her strongest skill, she feels as though the course and her professor, Ryan Mead, helped her to develop and strengthen her own unique writing style. Her overall experience in this course has shaped her to be a more confident and careful writer.

During the writing process, Rachel found it most difficult to select a topic that was both relevant and interesting. When beginning the Op-Ed essay, she suggests exploring possible topics as soon as the essay is assigned. Based on her own experience, she suggests that it is much more beneficial to choose a topic that is important to you, or else it will be challenging to remain engaged while writing the paper. But once you find that topic that you are passionate about, writing will come naturally.

Though Rachel is not currently registered in any writing courses, she looks forward to applying the skills she learned in Writing 111 in the future.

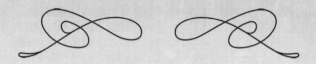

SEXUAL ASSAULT: HOW TO PROTECT THOSE PROTECTING US

Rachel Willison

Professor Ryan Mead

"It was fight or flight, and I flew," states Brenda Hoster, a former sergeant major of the Army, when she recalls her experiences with sexual assault in the military (Carpenter). Like Hoster, many women in the military are victims of sexual assault, but unlike Hoster, who after a long period of time was brave enough to report her attacker, many fail to report the crime. In 2012, an estimated 26,000 military personnel had been sexually assaulted, but only a fraction of this number came forward and testified (Cassata and Lardner). So why are so few offenses being reported? Fear: victims lack confidence in the military's current judiciary system to act in properly prosecuting the perpetrator, and to protect them from retribution for accusing one of their own. Where does this lack of confidence originate? Is it not our government's duty to protect those defending our home? In recent efforts to combat sexual assault and to restore the safety and confidence in our soldiers, the U.S. Senate passed the National Defense Authorization Act (NDAA), and voted in favor of one of two bills proposed regarding the individual who presides over a sexual assault trial. Will the redistribution of power eliminate unwillingness to report, or will it cause trust issues in other aspects of the commander-subordinate relationship? These reforms have yet to establish full confidence in reporting among service women. Shouldn't we attempt to build this trust by educating our officers about sexual assault, and train them how to address as well as prevent the issue? Our government should take responsibility and establish a sexual assault prevention education requirement for all military personnel.

The government has not completely neglected its responsibilities to protect our servicewomen against sexual assault. At the close of 2013, the U.S. government passed the revised National Defense Authorization Act for the 2014 fiscal year that included 30 reforms relating to sexual offenses in the military (McKeon). Effective laws and limitations employed through these reforms include stripping commanders' authority to dismiss findings by court martial and reducing guilty findings, allowing unit transfers for the victims of sexual assault, and the removal of perpetrators from service temporarily or permanently (McKeon). These innovative reforms of the NDAA are not convincing the Senate that they are enough. As John Barrasso, Wisconsin representative, expresses: "I think the National Defense Authorization Act has done a significant amount; it could go further" (Kaper).

Therefore it is evident government awareness of this issue is present, but is government action? In effort to take the fight against sexual assault further, New York senator Kristen Gillibrand proposed a bill to senate that would ultimately remove the power to prosecute from commanders and place it in the hands of independent, trained, professional military prosecutors. This bill would restore to service members and victims confidence in the justice system to report rape and receive fair trial. But during the voting process on the bill, many members presented the argument that this would undermine the hierarchy of power between the commanders and their troops. So, in order to avoid disrupting this precious hierarchy—that seems determinate to the proper functioning of the army—yet still establish trust, the guilty party must restore their credibility through necessary education.

While it seems apparent that the distrust originates in the power held by commanders concerning the criminal prosecution process, properly educating officers could rebuild trust. Specifically, according to AP research, on a military base in Japan, only one third of those found guilty of committing offenses are actually receiving penalty ("Senate Must Pass Reforms"). It can be inferred that the commanding officers conducting these trials are not administering the necessary punishment because they are not qualified to determine the appropriate repercussions. Disappointing statistics like this, to say the least, rapidly discourage victims to uphold their cases. Qualifications to properly indict a case must first be administered to encourage victims to confidently rely on their officers to represent them.

Ultimately Gillibrand's bill was vetoed 55-45 by the Senate's final vote on March 6, leaving the issue unresolved (Cassata and Lardner). Thus, fellow senator Claire McCaskill, an advocate for the chain of command, proposed an alternative sexual assault bill that allows the victim to choose whether a military prosecutor or the commanding officer presides over the case (Cassata and Lardner). This more conservative proposal won overwhelmingly in the senate; however, it does not address the problem of victims' apprehension and skepticism. This bill affirms that commanders maintain the same influence over their subordinates, so what is to stop victims from being harassed for not choosing their commander to prosecute the case? Under these circumstances coercion still fails to be eliminated; it instead is simply redirected. If not chosen to preside over the case, it is a poor reflection of the commander's ability to lead his troops. In reality a commander's ability to lead is, in fact, in question due to the lack of experience or knowledge in the field of sexual assault. This problem could be solvable if the attainment of this knowledge is enforced. Yet victims are still faced with the difficult choice between a properly educated lawyer, and possible harassment for making that choice, and a commanding officer who lacks experience and knowledge, in order to avoid harassment.

Admittedly, who would choose their commanding officer, when given the choice, over a professional? In addition to the dismal conviction statistics like those tallied by AP, commanders are not trained in sexual assault cases. Odds like these would cause errors that ultimately produce doubt in the abilities of the military courtroom. If the government were to require a workshop to educate commanding officers in the different types and severities of sexual assault, they would be better qualified to take the position of prosecutor. Incorporating this sexual assault education workshop in officer training and in the progression of ranks would solidify the importance of military sexual safety. It would not only improve credibility in the courtroom, but boost the confidence of sexual assault victims of being treated justly.

McCaskill's bill stresses the credibility held by commanding officers. Sexual assault instruction would not only maintain military credibility but improve it. Education would conserve the pre-determined authority established by a commander's title while building confidence. As a commander you are liable for the actions and safety of your unit and by not instituting any change of the commanders' role in a sexual assault case, McCaskill's bill ameliorates discrepancies in their responsibilities. The proposal that allows victims to decide who presides over their case does address the increasingly contagious plague of distrust. But it only scrapes the surface of the issue; we still need to dig deeper and address the root of the problem: the military's overall comprehension of what is understood as sexual assault.

In fact, in preparation for the sexual assault debate, the male-dominated military population's awareness and comprehension of sexual assault was put to question. Gillibrand, who actively questioned joint chiefs of staff with the members of the Senate Armed Services Committee, stated: "Not every single commander believes what a sexual assault is. Not every single commander can distinguish between a slap on the ass and a rape because they merge all of these crimes together" (Cassata and Lardner). Though both are forms of sexual harassment, the inability to distinguish between a major crime and a minor offense leaves the question how women are to confidently report.

Through the education of those responsible for administering justice among their ranks, we can restore this lost confidence. Commanders need to be held accountable for the ongoing problem of sexual assault and education is one way to achieve this. Government institution of a mandatory sexual assault awareness course would enlighten the uninformed commanding officer of the magnitude of the problem present in their institution. There are already a few programs that offer training in sexual assault prevention such as the SHARP (Sexual Harassment/Assault Response & Prevention) program. But programs like these are optional. Individuals who are not educated about sexual assault are unaware of their ignorance, and therefore will not branch out and seek knowledge. Thus it must be emphasized that instruction is a requirement enforced by the government.

The United States is aware of the longstanding issue threatening the safety of our servicewomen. The government has engaged in intervention through reforms and the passage of bills. But sexual offenses are still occurring in astonishing numbers, and more shocking is the number that go unreported. Trust needs to be built within the military's chain of command to effectively lower these statistics. The Senate's hesitancy to devalue commanding authority leaves doubt in the mind of the victims. In order not to disturb the current equilibrium of power and, more importantly, to protect those risking their lives to protect us, education must be administered. Education throughout training will avoid belittling a commanders' position and strengthen it in the eyes of their subordinates, thus eliminating the threat of misrepresentation and harassment. Service member safety is a commander's responsibility and it is our responsibility to provide the tools for them to fulfill their duties.

Works Cited

Cassata, Donna and Richard Lardner. "Senate Blocks Change to Military Sex Assault Cases." *Washington Times*. Washington Times, 6 Mar. 2014. Web. 7 Mar. 2014.

Carpenter, Zoe. "20 Years Ago, an Army Veteran Reported a Sexual Assault. She's Still Waiting for Justice." *The Nation*. The Nation, 24 Feb. 2014. Web. 13 Mar. 2014.

Kaper, Stacy. "Why Is Kristen Gillibrand's Military Sexual-Assault Bill Stalled Out?" *The Atlantic*. Edgecast Networks, 13 Jan. 2014. Web. 9 Mar. 2014.

McKeon, Buck. *FY 2014 National Defense Authorization Act*. Armed Services Committee, HR.1960. S.1197. Rept. 2013. 9 Dec. 2013. Web. 15 Mar. 2014.

"Senate must pass reforms to help end epidemic of sexual assault military." Editorial. *San Jose Mercury News*. Mercury News, 12 Feb. 2014. Web. 7 Mar. 2014.

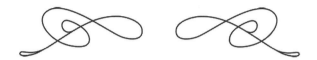

RESEARCHED ARGUMENTS

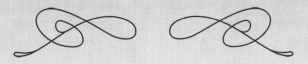

Yafen Huang

From Ridgewood, New York, Yafen is a School of Management student majoring in Accounting. Outside the world of numbers, writing is one of the best ways for Yafen to relieve stress. She sees writing as an escape, a way to express her feelings, and a world where she can fully be herself. Her other hobbies include playing guitar, taking naps on lazy afternoons, and spending quality time with friends and family.

The research paper first appeared to be Yafen's least favorite writing assignment when the professor handed out the syllabus to the class. However, as she started the process of researching and integrating resources to create an academic debate, her attitude toward the research paper switched from negative to positive. Though the writing was very challenging and time-consuming, Yafen had enjoyed developing her own researched argument on the ecological footprint. She believed that the essence of a researched argument is to find a topic that the writer would ultimately find interesting and care about. Deprived of such passion, the process would be boring and frustrating. With an interesting topic, the researched argument will be compelling to both the audience and the writer.

Writing 111 was Yafen's third and so far her favorite writing class in Binghamton. It provided her a chance to deeply explore herself through the personal statement and learned how to develop both civil and informative tone on the research paper. Her experience with Professor Jennifer Sweeney was also very involving. Throughout the process of drafting and revising, Yafen was always welcome to reach out for advice. Great ideas would spark during the conversation, and by the time the meeting was over, she would feel fully inspired and ready to move on to the next step of writing.

ECOLOGICAL FOOTPRINT: THE INDICATOR OF OVER-DEMANDING HUMANITY

Yafen Huang

Professor Jen Sweeney

Imagine your monthly income is $1500. You use most of it each month on food, rent, all the other necessities and sometimes even go over the budget by swiping your credit card for an extra luxury. Then one day, you are fired. Your income is totally cut off and you might even end up in debt. That hypothetical situation is exactly what we are doing to our planet. With the increasing global population and economic development, over-reliance on the planet's ecological services and natural resources has become inevitable. There's no doubt that human economy depends on the earth's natural capital. Everything that we demand takes away from this planet. Yet, what's more terrifying is that we cannot negotiate with nature. There's no credit card or loan we can take and then repay nature later.

To understand the purpose of our demands and to protect future generations' economic and social wellbeing, we must use a practical tool to analyze the relationship between nature and humanity. In my paper, I will use Ecological Footprint (hereafter EF) as a practical indicator to reveal the "land-grabbing" humanity and the importance of maintaining sustainable development through the management of ecological assets (Wackernagle and Rees). Though there are critics who challenge the practicality of EF and fear that its calculation might be misleading and confusing, I still maintain that EF is a realistic and practical concept in presenting the relationship between human activities and environmental deficit on both a global and local scale. It is necessary to have a clear overview on modern environmental issues in order to understand the cause and effect of our actions. In this case, EF helps us achieve this understanding from a perspective that presents calculations in simple units yet at the same time provides a greater meaning.

Using EF as an accounting tool for sustainability not only simplifies the complexity in our ecosystem, but also presents the most straightforward way for us to see what kind of challenge we are facing: "humanity is at or beyond global carry capacity" as the founders of the concept Wackernagle and Rees originally proposed. First introduced in the 1990s, the EF was aimed to measure the impacts of human activity on the ecosystem for the benefit of protecting the well-being of humans and our natural heritage (Blomqvist). The basic concept behind this measurement is that the earth has only a limited amount of bio-productive land as well as finite natural resources to supply human demands. To maintain a sustainable development, humans must live within nature's restrained carrying capacity. The EF is an aggregated indicator measured in a standardized area unit expressed in global hectares per capita (gha/cap), where "global hectare" quantifies the average bio-capacity of earth in one year (Collins and Flynn). The calculation of EF estimates the area of lands that is required to support a defined population's consumption in a given year. This consumption includes the population's needs for food and drink, domestic energy such as electricity, and gas. Comparing the estimated area to the available bio-capacity, we will have a clear view of the imbalance between human demand and natural supply.

One of the most widely-known results from the EF calculation is that "humanity currently uses the equivalent of 1.5 Earths to support human needs" (Blomqvist). Thereby, actions taken by human activities have already formed the modern phenomena of "ecological overshoot," indicating humans are exceeding the regenerative capacity of earth's ecosystem. A recent report released from the Global Footprint Network reveals that earth's capacity in 2008 was 12 billion hectares while humanity's footprint was 18.2 billion. The average ecological footprint reached 2.7 gha/cap compared to only 1.8 gha of available lands (Wackernagle and Rees). This phenomenon of "ecological overshoot" leads to severe consequences such as the rapid increase of greenhouse gases in the atmosphere, abnormal climate change, ocean acidification and the loss of biodiversity due to the massive human constructions. To measure such over-demanding human activities, EF has been verified as one of the most useful approaches in demonstrating the damages driven by human activities as a tool of calculation and communication. Numerous applications have been taken place in various countries and were performed successfully by different organizations, services and governments (Collins and Flynn 299).

However, despite the international recognition of EF, there are still critics questioning whether or not the measurement of EF is practical in terms of the local scale. This critique revolves around the concern that EF takes in all the data and converts them into fixed units without considering the variability between local regions and the global scale as a whole. Van Kooten and Bulte conclude that EF puts all globally available data into a single metric, causing its measurement to be unclear and inflexible as well as leading to the failure on calling effective political actions in the local community. They argue, "Beyond rhetoric to limit consumption, which is naïve and politically unacceptable notion, there is no policy prescription" in EF (388). Yet this statement isn't valid because there are applications where local government adjusts EF from a global scale into the local environmental policy agenda.

A case study conducted by the Cardiff County Council (CCC) proved to be one of the most successful examples integrating the local-global connection using EF in the UK. The CCC's goals were to bring sustainable development into the decision-making process, raise local residents' awareness toward sustainability and assess Cardiff's impacts on the environment (Collins and Flynn 302). During the process of collecting and analyzing data that is specified in Cardiff, all of the information was transparent and engaged with key council officials in regards to keeping all the materials open and legitimate. Regulated progress reports prepared by researchers were also presented to policy makers periodically in order to keep them involved with the whole project. Based on the past experiences with EF in other UK regions, the main issues with its application were the lack of data transparency and the failure of generating political commitment toward the data collection (Collins and Flynn 301). However, the Cardiff project overcame these problems by having open corporate research, which allows officers to be involved and motivated. These factors ultimately led to the success of selling the EF to different level of policy makers and transformed the Cardiff research study into practical policy decision.

The final results indicate that the overall EF for Cardiff was 1.72 million global hectares and the average of 5.59 global hectares per resident. As the capital city of Wales, Cardiff has a higher average than both UK (5.35 ghp/cap) and Welsh residents (5.25 gha/cap) (Collins and Flynn 307). With these few simple statistics, the Cardiff EF project gives the simplest yet strongest evidence to show how local residents' consumption over-demands ecological resources in comparison with Wales and other UK regions. This evidence helps policy makers to recognize the value of EF and further encourages them to rethink ways to help the community utilize resources sustainably. Suggested policies include "consuming more organic and seasonal food and drink; generating energy from renewable sources such as solar, wind and tidal;…considering the resource use and impact of a development over its lifetime; and considering the ecological impacts in planning and managing events" (Collins and Flynn 309). As Cardiff local agencies continue to use EF to monitor residents' ecological impact and adjust their policy to maintain a sustainable environment, this application of EF successfully shows how it is realistic and practical to use EF in local areas. Furthermore, it strikes political interest as well as promotes residents' efforts by raising the importance of limiting unnecessary consumption.

Another critical argument that questions the credibility of EF measurement is that although it concludes humans have exceeded the planet's carrying capacity and the world is experiencing ecological deficit, is such a finding necessarily a bad thing? From the perspective of Blomqvist et al, "EF measurement, as currently constructed and presented, is so misleading as to preclude their use in any serious science or policy context." Kooten and Bulte point out that the ecological deficit, which is equivalent to 'overshooting' (when EF is greater than nature carrying capacity) can be an indicator showing the growth of economic development, and may even be "optimal in the sense of increasing overall well-being": they reject the claim that overshooting is an absolutely bad thing (388). For example, they argue converting forests into productive plantations can be beneficial due to plantations' greater agricultural output. In their words, as EF assumes that the current stock of natural resources is somehow optimal, then therefore "there is no reason why depleting some of it may not be optimal" (Kooten and Bulte 388). In that case, it's okay for one to have a larger footprint. However, this assumption that "it's okay to consume" ignores the terrifying impacts that, when all human activities are added up together, they leave destructive effects on environment as a whole and worsen as time goes on.

A Norwegian case study conducted in 2007 is a perfect example and proves the flaw in the assumption. The original hypothesis made by researchers from the Norwegian case stated that high-consuming industrialized countries such as Norway experience decreasing sustainability in environmental production as human consumption increased (Aall and Husabo 3624). The final results support this hypothesis through the application of EF as well. With the steady increase in population and common wealth, Norwegians are more able to afford goods and services. As the demands of goods and services grow, the rise of consumption eventually eliminates the bonus of eco-efficiency in production, causing the reduction in sustainability.

The Norwegian case study compares the environmental impact of production and consumption in Norway from 1987 to 2007 using EF as a calculation tool. Similar to the Cardiff project, the underlying purpose of this case is also to trigger government officials to push sustainable consumption issues as priorities among the agenda of Norwegian politicians (Aall and Husabo 3625). In order to put the main focus on the consumption aspect, the Norwegian researchers constructed the application of EF into six steps when collecting and processing the data. Their first step is to convert the amount of consumption in monetary or physical units. The second through fifth steps are to assess land use, energy use, energy-related GHG emissions (greenhouse gas emission), and non-energy related emissions relating to or caused by Norwegian consumption. The last step is then to calculate Norway's ecological footprint based on the findings of steps two to five (Aall and Husabo 3626). Through the use of EF, the study results illustrate the striking impact that over the period of 1987 to 2006, the size of Norway's ecological footprint had increased by 12% because of the rising consumption within the country's border. Another alarming finding is that over the same time period, with the globally increasing population, the available global bio-productive lands also declined by 24%. This means that with the reduction in the overall bio-productive area, the ecological footprint per capita of Norwegian consumption is actually 33% more over the past 19 years (3631).

The most important outcome of the Norwegian case is that through calculation it is easy to see why the size of both production and consumption matters. As Aall and Husabo conclude, "what matters here is not the moderate increase in the size of ecological footprint in Norway (and similar countries) over the last 20 years, but rather the fact that the footprint could have been much smaller in these two decades if we had allowed increased production efficiency to benefit the environment" (3634). In this case, they refer "production efficiency" to products like hybrid cars. They offer the argument that because humans consume resources that are easiest to obtain, such as the commonly used fuel gas cars, eco-efficiency is bound to decline due to the given volume of consumption. As the dramatic increase in transportation in Norway contributes the main compositions of greenhouse gas emission, local air pollution and energy use, it is fair to state that the choice of consumption heavily influences the size of ecological footprint. Aall and Husabo suggest a solution by proposing that instead of monitoring the impact caused by human consumption, it is more useful to develop a specific consumption focus in policy making, which they call "consumption-oriented environmental policy" (3635). This means that rather than saying "it's okay to consume," it's wiser to filter certain types of products to consume rather than goods that would enlarge the size of EF even more. With the knowledge of what to consume, we can ensure the continuous growth of economy and shift consumption in a more sustainable direction at the same time.

A speech titled "The need to create more green jobs" given during the United Nations Climate Change Conference in Copenhagen 2009 by the chief Norwegian negotiator states the following: "By 2050 we must have reached the goal of zero-emissions—and I believe we must acknowledge that it is foolhardy to expect people to cut off the very limb on which they stand. We cannot convince people to stop consuming" (Aall and Husabo 3636). This statement is true. Humans consume, and as the population grows, consumption will also only climb on a positive trend. Writers like Veen and Opschoor, two experts in the field of environmental and spatial economics, similarly suggested that by converting human consumption from a monetary unit to a biophysical unit, the use of EF effectively addresses the importance of "awareness" (Veen). Opschoor further concludes that "the environmental impact of a country's economic activity is the accumulated sum of environmental changes that its level of consumption gives rise to" (Opschoor 363). This again emphasizes the strong correlation between consumption level and the damage to nature. Though it is very difficult to give up our desire to demand and consume, we must have a realistic picture of what is our position in ecological terms. As more environmentalists, socialists, and even economists continue to explore the possibilities of maintaining proficient utilization, it is also our responsibility to take a step back and think of what exactly we want as individuals. Shall we enjoy the luxury now and leave a place where there are no more accessible resources for our future generations, or is it wiser to slow down our pace so we can access better management of our ecological capital?

The ultimate purpose of using EF as a tool to estimate the relationship between human action and natural resources is not to conclude that we should stop all our consumption. By incorporating Ecological Footprint in policy making, it extends our understanding of human impacts and further encourages us to take deeper consideration of what kind of resources to utilize in ways that maximize the benefit of both societal and environmental development. The solution to the problem is easy—as long as we maintain a simpler and less expensive lifestyle, we will benefit from having more leisure time and greater health (Onisto, Wackernagel, Bello, et al). It is possible for us to pursue common welfare without sacrificing our homelands. After all, humanity is not all about spending, but also saving.

Works Cited

Aall, C., and Husabo, I. "Is Eco-Efficiency a Sufficient Strategy for Achieving a Sustainable Development? The Norwegian Case." *Sustainability 2* (2010): 3623–3638. *MDPI.com* Web. April 20, 2014.

Bastianoni, Niccolucci, et al. "Sustainable Development: Ecological Footprint in Accounting." *Encyclopedia of Environment Management.* (May 2013): 2467–2481. *Taylor & Francis online.* Web. March 31, 2014.

Blomqvist, Linus, Barry W. Brook, et al. "Does the Shoe Fit? Real Versus Imagined Ecological Footprints." *PLoS Biol.* N.p. November 2013. Web. March 31, 2014.

Collins, A. and Flynn, A. "Engaging with the Ecological Footprint as a Decision-Making Tool: Process and Responses." *Local Environment* (June 2007): 295–312. *Taylor & Francis Online.* Web. April 3, 2014.

Kooten, G. and Bulte, E. "The ecological footprint: useful science or politics?" *Ecological Economics 32* (2000): 385–389. *Elsevier.com.* Web. April 3, 2014.

Onisto, L., Wackernagel, M., Bello, P., et al. "National natural capital accounting with the ecological footprint concept." *Ecological Economics 29* (June 1999): 375–390. *Elsevier.com.* Web. April 23, 2014.

Opschoor, Hans. "The ecological footprint: measuring rod or metaphor?" *Ecological Economics 32* (2000): 363–365. *Elsevier.com.* Web. April 24, 2014.

Wackernagel, M. and Rees, W. "The Shoe Fits, but the Footprint is Larger than Earth." *PLoS Biol.* N.p. November 2013. Web. March 31, 2014.

van der Veen, Anne. *Ecological Footprint (EF)* N.p N.d. Web. April 3, 2014.

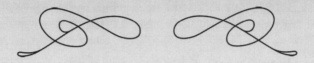

Erick Martinez, Jr.

Erick Martinez, Jr. was born and raised in Bronx, New York. He is currently undeclared with an interest in studying Computer Science and minoring in Mathematics. In his spare time, he enjoys graphic design, drawing, and photography.

Erick found that writing his researched argument was the most time consuming and stressful of the three assignments, but also the most rewarding. Finding a topic that interested him and was unique was one of the hardest parts in writing his research argument. The other challenging part was organizing his sources and figuring out which ones to use. The actual research made for the most enjoyable part in the writing of his essay. Learning new things on current topics that interested him allowed him to express easier. His philosophy on writing is to always start early and get feedback.

Erick believes that Writing 111 contributed a lot to his growth as a college writer. His 111 teacher was Jennifer Sweeney and his advice to students new to college writing is to get a lot of feedback on your essays. The peer revision in class played a good part in the revision of his essays. He also strongly suggests that you go to the writing center and your teacher's office hours for help on your essays because any form of constructive criticism is valuable to a college writer. His last suggestion is to write about something you are passionate or interested in—it makes the process a lot smoother.

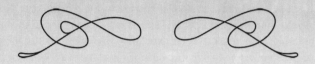

SEXISM AND VIDEO GAMES: A BETTER FUTURE

Erick Martinez, Jr.

Professor Jen Sweeney

In recent years, the influence of video games as an interactive medium has rapidly moved to homes of millions through the world. Like any form of media, Video Games (VG) have been shown to affect the way people perceive themselves and others. The video game industry has also, for a long time, been considered a male domain—an unrestricted sanctum for males to express themselves in ways they would not be able to offline. Many people within the video game community believe that women who claim video games are sexist are either lying, being too sensitive, or exaggerating stories. However, actual evidence disproving the existence of the pandemic of sexism has not been presented. The harsh reality is that the influence of the video games on society has long been underestimated and understudied; these games have now been proven to have short-term effects on gamers' cognition, self-esteem, and behavioral tendencies. I will demonstrate through my own research that the video game industry has been perpetuating negative gender attitudes towards women. These attitudes have influenced all areas of the video game industry including the workplace, the gaming community, and even the marketing and development of video games themselves. I will also examine the effects of the gaming industry's sexism, its ties to toxic and vitriolic online gaming interactions, and the many myths surrounding women and their interests in gaming culture.

Video games have been an escapist outlet for years, but have been recently surrounded with a ton of controversy, especially around the topic of sexism within the industry. In the short history of VGs, the culture has amassed millions of followers and has become a billion-dollar industry. According to Jesse Fox, an assistant professor at Ohio State University and researcher on the effects of new media, children between the ages of 8 and 18 spend an average of almost three hours daily on VGs and computers combined. One thing to note is that the majority of research on VG culture has been on its effect on society and the correlation between violent VGs and violence in the real world. Cara Ellison, a writer and video game critic, argues that even the relation of the fantasy of virtual worlds to real life "infantilizes" the subculture of gaming. Such criticism overlooks that the way VGs are marketed and how people interact with each other in these virtual worlds, and the pervasive contents of the games being created all affect real people and a lot of people outside of the subculture of gaming don't know anything about it. In arguing this claim, writer Laura Bates, a founder of the "Everyday Sexism Project"—a compilation of tens of thousands women's daily experiences with gender equality—argues that it is a case of art imitating real-life gender imbalance; VGs and the people making them are perpetuating those imbalances. Therefore, imposing sexualized material on the public effectively normalizes sexist beliefs and thoughts.

In a recent empirical study, Jennifer Allaway, a writer for game developer magazine *Gamasutra* and social researcher on the game industry, discusses sexism in the industry with the use of statistical evidence, anecdotes, and verbal representations of sexism and harassment in the VG industry. Allaway's methodology for her research included a survey of 48 questions posted online through various platforms, which resulted in the collection of 344 anonymous responses (60% male and 40% female) representing wage, age, and ethnic diversity. In order to give you a better context of some of the covert and overt sexism that occurs in the industry, one subject in Allaway's research recalled that, "At some point you just become, well not desensitized, but you grow numb to it [sexism], because it's the same thing every week. You know, 'This is isolated, this isn't representative of systemic problems', those two can get you feeling pretty numb. It's not just a numbness of, 'I feel nothing', it's also the numbness of I can do nothing, I feel totally powerless." Such powerlessness suggests that more sexism is going on than is actually being reported in the industry. The fear of being blackballed or fired keeps women from voicing their concern, effectively strengthening sexism, especially in a male-dominated industry.

Allaway shows that wage gaps and glass ceilings for women, larger cultural problems, are also integral problems in the industry. In the gaming industry, most women don't even reach the glass ceiling because of the reinforced power dynamic that discourages women to advance to stay in the industry. Allaway's work shows that "59.2% of women disagreed with the statement that men's and women's voices are respected equally during meetings at work, compared to 33.6% of men. Women were three times as likely (30.8%) as men (10.3%) to notice a glass ceiling in their company." These saddening statistics show that more than one in three women in the industry experience or suspect a wage gap (Allaway). Given the relatively recent, controversial revelation of sexism in video game culture, Allaway's research provides essential groundwork for the discussion of sexism in the gaming community and possible solutions for a more gender-inclusive future.

Further, Allaway discusses the probable cause for overt sexism in the industry, which she calls covert sexism, i.e., sexism not openly shown or acknowledged that, once accepted in the work environment—"the rape jokes, the constant sprawl of sexed-up female characters, the boys' club culture—[enables] overt sexism...to develop." This assertion is backed up with the statistic that "69.3% of women and 44.4% of men admit that at least one colleague has acted in a way that they found offensive on the basis of gender." The amount of sexual discrimination in the industry and online gaming has resulted from covert industrial sexism that trickles down through their products reinforcing gender norms and stereotypical roles. The inferences of this occurring are justified through Allaway's work and Jennifer Jenson's article, "Tipping Points: Marginality, Misogyny, and Videogames."

Jennifer Jenson demonstrates in her that article the "conditions of precarity that women face as marginal subjects in the video games industry and as sexualized objects in the creative and cultural projects that the world's largest entertainment industry produces." Jenson analyzes two popular cases of harassment that would otherwise be considered criminally offensive if done offline (in the real world) as opposed to being under the disguise of anonymity (in the internet). One of the cases pertains to Jennifer Hepler, a Bioware developer, and one to Anita Sarkeesian, a feminist, media critic, and creator of a series of videos, "Feminist Frequency," analyzing women's portrayals within pop culture. Both were sexually harassed to the point where they had to change their numbers; a video game was created of Sarkeesian which allowed the player to beat her up. These cases are vital to the equality movement and debate on sexism because they are what got the media talking. Through her easily accessible online documentation, Jenson's article also raises awareness on the prevalence of online sexism and misogynistic attitudes.

The number of women currently working in the industry is almost directionally proportional to the meaningful representation of them (i.e., not objectified or overly-sexualized) as leading characters in advertisements, box-arts, and the games themselves. From a historical standpoint, VGs weren't always socially and culturally a masculine field. In her article "Why Marketers Fear the Female Geek," Anjin Anhut, a video game blogger, examines how games effectively work to exclude women from their intended demographic. The idea is that women were originally a part of the intended audience but through target group optimization (a marketing technique used to maximize the return on the marketing budget) women were eventually excluded because few women would buy the games. The message is then optimized for a new audience through another very common marketing technique Anhut calls, "messaging optimization," a method in which the marketers sell their product by telling the target group they are superior to the excluded group (women, in this case). Then once other companies see this "working" sexism, a systemic piggyback effect occurs, thus perpetuating the cycle of exclusion. The final idea is that once you create this superior product, you segregate the market to still make profit off the excluded market by making a product that does not contradict your original brand's message. All of this based on the myth that "that women somehow inherently are not into science, tech, comics, games and other geek stuff" (Anhut); a myth that helps perpetuate gender imbalance.

Anhut proposes a solution to the vicious cycle of excluding women called, "*disruptive innovation*," a term that describes an innovation that goes against common best practices and succeeds. A noteworthy statistic from EEDAR, the leading provider of VG research, showed that, "[Out of] a sample of 669 action games, shooters, and RPGs, all taken from the seventh-generation console cycle (that's Xbox 360, PS3, and Wii—in other words, everything in the last seven years), less than 300 games...had the option of a female lead. As for female only leads...a whopping 24." Out of the sample size, games with a female option statistically sold 25 percent less than games with exclusively a male hero. In addition to these male-only hero games selling 75 percent more than the female-only led games (Chambers). These shocking statistics amplify the issue of budgets on female protagonist-led games, which are significantly fewer than male-led ones. The only two things that are needed to allow disruptive innovation to succeed is support of the practice and creating a demand for it.

That women are excluded from marketing functions reinforces the reality that VGs also underrepresent and objectify women in the games themselves. An academic study conducted at Clark College suggests that pretty much everyone aside from white males are marginalized in VGs (Dickerman et al. 2008). The study briefly touches on the difference between the portrayals of women in game advertisements versus those in the actual game. Some examples include: "Neverwinter Nights" (2002) and "Sid Meier's: Civilization V" (2007), which both have advertisements centered on a nearly naked woman and the Statue of Liberty, respectively. In the "Neverwinter Nights" case, the woman used in the advertisement was clothed less than in the actual game. In Sid Meier's advertisement, headlined "CIV GOES BIG," the Statue of Liberty was given a larger than normal bust. But in reality, the games have nothing overtly sexual about them. When companies operate under the assumption that women are not interested in games, they maintain the cycle of the pervasive gender roles that have been prevalent for decades.

Paul Stermer and Melissa Burkley, researchers at Oklahoma State University engage the idea in their article "Xbox or SeXbox?" that sexism is prevalent in VG culture. The article highlights the prevalence of sexualized content in VGs and its connection to sexist attitudes towards women in the gaming culture. Stermer and Burkley use their research to examine how the sexualized content has increased over the years in not only advertisement, but also in the games themselves. They question how much pervasive objectifying material can affect real world perceptions of both men and women: "exposure to sexualized VG content has been shown to increase gender stereotyping, facilitate the accessibility of sexist thoughts, produce greater tolerance for sexual harassment and decrease players' body self-esteem." Iowa State University's Chistopher Barlett also demonstrates short-term negative effects on player's self-esteem after playing VGs, thus emphasizing the gender norm for males and females. Although Barlett's study only proves the short-term effects, constant exposure to videogames has shown to be related to changes in adolescent personalities according to a meta-analytic review done by eight university researchers (Anderson et al. 2010).

Some argue that the sexy content in games is needed because nobody wants to see or play men in revealing and sexualized costumes. This argument is more of a personal concern and points to self-esteem issues in some of the vocal consumer demographic. The over sexualized content as a result of a sexist VG culture has limited the growth of the industry and its products, whose creativity is limited because of the sexist boundary placed by VG culture.

Consumption and exposure to this kind of media was confirmed to have a variety of effects on consumers. One study by Yao et al, a group of researchers from three different universities, confirmed that by playing objectifying games, men were more likely to view women as sexual objects in real life, think more about sex, and exhibit more self-proclaimed tendencies to act indecently around women in real life (Yao). Yao reached these results by having 74 male players play a rated-mature game titled "LeisureSuit Larry: Magna cum Laude" against two control games ("The Sims" and "Pacman II"). The results provided proof of some of the effects on how games can affect people in real life.

Another way that video games have shown to affect people is through a phenomenon known as the Proteus effect, which simply shows that under the guise of an avatar, one either displays individual behaviors that differ from their normal behaviors in real life or that they become very similar. In his article in *Slate* magazine discussing his book *The Proteus Paradox: How Online Games and Virtual Worlds Change Us—And How They Don't*, Nick Yee concludes that virtual worlds are authentic. Hal Hershfield, a professor at New York University's Stern School of Business, uses digital doppelgängers (digital replicas) of college students aged 40 years and found that those same students, in Yee's words, "were more willing to put aside money given a hypothetical windfall." Yee uses his own research and Hal Hershfield's virtual doppelgänger experiment results to prove what he calls the "Proteus effect," the phenomena where our digital avatars can change our behaviors and how we perceive things. Yee's connections between gender bending and gender stereotyping show that virtual worlds do indeed perpetuate the status quo (Yee). The focus of the article zooms in when he talks about how the government uses virtual worlds like "America's Army" for recruitment into the army, which has been proven to be one of their most successful recruitment tools (Yee). This connection and discovery is important because it means that the government is starting to see the cultural significance of the online gaming community and because it denies the common misconception that VGs do not have an effect on real life behaviors.

Outside of sexism on the industrial level, verbal abuse, sexist attitudes, and gender stereotyping has become a pervasive problem in first person shooters, one of gaming's most popular genres centered on gun-based combat through a first person perspective. Although verbal abuse is something all gamers face when venturing online, especially in voice chat, there's a vitriol reserved specifically for women (Chambers). An informative study by Jeffrey Kuznekoff & Lindsey Rose, two professors at Ohio State University, titled, "Communication in multiplayer gaming: Examining player responses to gender cues" addresses two major questions: "does player gender affect the types of comments received in-game, and is player skill a factor?" (Chambers). They conducted the research on Halo 3, a widely popular shooter game, because of its randomized matchmaking, finding that "on average, the female voice received three times as many negative comments as the male voice or no voice" (Kuznekoff & Rose). The outcome of the study is valuable because instead of collecting data on players in a lab environment, it evaluates player behaviors in their natural environment playing VGs voluntarily.

Although this makes the results more reliable, it doesn't make them light-hearted. The most surprising result I understood from Chambers' study was not that women were more likely to be verbally abused, an assumption I could infer from my own personal experience and years of online gaming. It was the correlation between the skill levels of the women and the amount of verbal harassment they received, which in turn had no effect on the amount of verbal abuse they received (Chambers). Chambers gives many examples of the kind of vitriolic language that was reserved for women online. According to her, on many occasions, even the slightest utterance made by women, even if positive, was quickly responded to with derogatory and offensive insults (Kuznekoff & Rose). This kind of language and verbal abuse is actually fairly common for men and women online, in addition to the "go make me a sandwich" or "fat, ugly, or slutty" remarks women online face a lot in games. It's important to note that although Koznekoff's study is only on the Halo 3 platform, the environment is extremely toxic and moderators have been shown to rarely enforce the rules against it with problematic players. The argument that men also get the same treatment as women online or that it's just trash talk, get over it doesn't hold up well using Kuznekoff's results because, although men do suffer from a lot of trash talk and verbal abuse, women are shown to receive three times as much. On top of that, the majority of it isn't warranted because Kuznekoff proved that skill plays no factor in the amount of harassment a women receives, which, as Chambers said, "indicates that something more than just a proclivity for trash-talk is at the core of this particular problem." The problem is that these same offenders participate in a culture that has normalized this kind of behavior for years and more times than not, continue to behave and hold the same views offline.

One of the major concepts my research shows is reflected in a quote by Jordan Shapiro, teacher at Temple University and researcher on the way video games help people interpret the world: "the industry will (and does) create games that simultaneously reflect and reinforce its own cultural attitudes around gender." Shapiro shares the same belief that VGs are not just for entertainment, but can be educational tools. Therefore, it is important to have an industry that is more inclusive and accepting of all genders, because of the effect of popular media on society. I believe that in order for change in the industry to occur, a new standard must be set. A standard in which women and men actually think critically about the normalized sexist behavior that often occurs and how it affects others.

Although sexism and the sexualization of women have been cultural problems for decades, that doesn't mean that it should be allowed to continue its vicious cycle in VG. Instead, the debate should be focused on more pressing issues like discrimination against women in the VG industry, the unpoliced domain of sexist attitudes, and the unchecked freedom to abuse people through the anonymity of the internet. Returning to Allaway, she provides some statistics that support this line of thought: "85.4% of women and 73.4% of men believe active gender inclusion will benefit the working environment of the game industry. 83.1% of women and 73.9% of men believe that the more diverse the workplace, the better the games the studio creates will be." We need to push for and support gender-inclusive games, mainstream feminist activism, and awareness of the actual prevalence of sexism. It is important to help end the pattern because media plays a tremendous part in our daily lives. Also, the people developing VGs have been reinforcing sexist attitudes and gender norms which trickle down to the consumers and perpetuate that. Like Yee suggested, although the solutions are simple, they won't happen easily. The best possible solution that covers many of the problems in VG culture would be *disruptive innovation* because it will allow for new a standard of gaming in the industry. That new standard will allow for more options and a brighter future for the gaming community.

Works Cited

Allaway, Jennifer. "The Reality of Sexism in the Game Industry." *Gamasutra*. UBM Tech web, 31 Mar. 2014. Web. 7 May 2014.

Anderson, Craig, Nobuko Ihori, Brad Bushman, Hannah Rothstein, Akiko Shibuya, Edward Swing, Akira Sakamoto, and Muniba Saleem. "Violent Video Game Effects on Aggression, Empathy, and Prosocial Behavior in Eastern and Western Countries: A Meta-Analytic Review." *Psychological Bulletin* 136.2 (2010): 151–73. Print.

Anhut, Anjin. "Why Marketers Fear The Female Geek." *Howtonotsuckatgamedesign.com.* 21 Dec. 2013. Web. 7 May 2014.

Barlett, Christopher P., and Richard J. Harris. "The Impact of Body Emphasizing Video Games on Body Image Concerns in Men and Women." *Sex Roles* 59.7–8 (2008): 586–601. 15 May 2008. Web. 11 Nov. 2014.

Bates, Laura. "Art Imitating Life: How Sexism in Video Games Mirrors Real-life Gender Imbalance." *The Independent*. Independent Digital News and Media, 4 Dec. 2012. Web. 10 Nov. 2014.

Chambers, Becky. "Academic Study Examines The Link Between Gender Cues and In-Game Harassment." *The Mary Sue*. 15 Feb. 2013. Web. 7 May 2014.

Chambers, Becky. "Why Games With Female Protagonists Don't Sell, and What It Says About The Industry." *The Mary Sue*. 23 Nov. 2012. Web. 8 May 2014.

Dickerman, Charles, Jeff Christensen, and Stella Beatríz Kerl-McClain. "Big Breasts and Bad Guys: Depictions of Gender and Race in Video Games." *Journal of Creativity in Mental Health* 3.1 (2008): 20–29. Academic Search Complete. Web. 7 May 2014.

Ellison, Cara. "There's No Sexism in Gaming." *New Statesman*. 8 July 2013. Web. 7 May 2014.

Fox, Jesse, and Wai Yen Tang. "Sexism in Online Video Games: The Role of Conformity to Masculine Norms and Social Dominance Orientation." *Computers in Human Behavior* 33 (2014): 151–73. *Elsevier*, 14 Apr. 2014. Web. 7 May 2014.

Jenson, Jennifer, and Suzanne De Castell. "Tipping Points: Marginality, Misogyny and Videogames." *Journal of Curriculum Theorizing* 29.2 (2013): 72–85. Web. 7 May 2014.

Kuznekoff, Jeffrey H., and Lindsey M. Rose. "Communication In Multiplayer Gaming: Examining Player Responses To Gender Cues." *New Media & Society* 15.4 (2013): 541–556. *Academic Search Complete*. Web. 7 May 2014.

Shapiro, Jordan. "#1ReasonWhy You Should Be Worried About Gender Equality in the Game Industry!" *Forbes*. Forbes Magazine, 29 Nov. 2012. Web. 7 May 2014.

Stermer, Paul S., and Melissa Burkley. "Xbox Or Sexbox? An Examination Of Sexualized Content In Video Games." *Social & Personality Psychology* 6.7 (2012): 525–535. *Academic Search Complete*. Web. 7 May 2014.

Walker, John. "Misogyny, Sexism, And Why RPS Isn't Shutting Up I Rock, Paper, Shotgun." *Rock Paper Shotgun*. 6 Apr. 2013. Web. 7 May 2014.

Yao, Mike, Chad Mahood, and Daniel Linz. "Sexual Priming, Gender Stereotyping, and Likelihood to Sexually Harass: Examining the Cognitive Effects of Playing a Sexually-Explicit Video Game." *Sex Roles* 62.1/2 (2010): 77–88. *Academic Search Complete*. Web. 7 May 2014.

Yee, Nick. "Why We Should Take Virtual Worlds Seriously." *Slate Magazine*. The Slate Group, 26 Jan. 2014. Web. 7 May 2014.

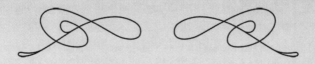

Gabrielle Sagesse

Gabrielle Sagesse is from Brooklyn, New York. She is an Integrative Neuroscience major with hopes of entering the medical field and becoming a pediatric oncologist. She is president of the Class of 2017 and a member of Charles Drew Minority Pre-Health Society. Gabrielle enjoys the sciences a lot, but also likes to just hang out with friends and relax.

Gabrielle attributes much of her growth and success as a writer to her Writing 111 instructor, Professor Sarah Seeley. Gabrielle chose to write her researched argument on a subject that is not only very dear to her but also culturally relevant. Gabrielle had a lot of fun writing her essay once she actually got into things. The hardest part for her, however, was revising the organization of the essay so it flowed smoothly. During the revision process, she visited her professor's office hours a lot, made appointments at the Writing Center, and consulted with her older sister Sabrina, who gave feedback on what parts were clear to her as someone who had not researched the subject, and which still needed clarification. She received an immense amount of help on her essay with the combination of these three resources.

Overall, Gabrielle had a great Writing 111 experience. Once she understood that no final draft is a finished draft, meaning that there is always still room for revision, she began to grow, and expand on her perspective of what good writing is. Gabrielle believes it is necessary to be ambitious with one's writing, be accepting of different views, and not to leave such writing to the last moment. A good essay needs time to be a good essay and for the writer not to be under stress.

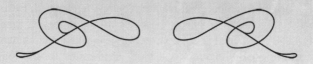

BLACK HAIR IN A WHITE WORLD: BLACK, WHITE, OR GRAY?

Gabrielle Sagesse

Professor Sarah Seeley

Issues associated with hair and beauty have long been a struggle for African American women. As a matter of fact, women from all over the globe can attest to the symbolic meaning of hair and the major role it plays in human societies. Hair is currently socially significant because it has the power to influence one's work life, divide races, and variously empower or disempower—the latter especially for African Americans. In an article entitled, "Why African American Women Try to Obtain 'Good Hair,'" author Whitney Bellinger examines the definitions of "good hair" versus "bad hair" according to African American women in order to understand the reasons these women change their hair from its supposed "natural state" (63). These views of hair can be seen as part of a racially underpinned hierarchy of the standards of beauty that must be met by women of color in order to survive in America. Furthermore, the idea of "good hair" and "bad hair" has created an environment of insecurity and psychological suppression for women of color. And while some people may believe hair is just hair, since slavery, hair for the black community has been a reflection of one's social status and identity. Hence, the willingness and unwillingness to wear hair naturally raises interesting questions. Is it a test of ethnic pride, as depicted during the Black Power Movement, or is hair just a commodity with no regards to self? Is wearing one's hair natural in a white world seen as rebellious, or is there a middle ground? Should black hair have to conform to the white standard of beauty? The way one chooses to wear their hair in the black community plays a prominent role in their social survival as it is portrayed historically, in the question of professionalism, and in class divisions.

Perceptions of beauty serve as a racial divider and evidence of a persistent form of structural racism. Tracey Patton, author of "Hey Girl, Am I More than My Hair?: African American Women and Their Struggles with Beauty, Body Image, and Hair," notes that beauty is subject to the influential standards of the ruling class (25). In this context, being beautiful means having "good hair." According to Bellinger, "good hair" is modeled on the long, wavy, straight, soft, manageable hair of Northern European women, while "bad hair"—short, kinky, frizzy, tightly coiled, woolly, and rough in nature—was equated with dark skinned races (65). More directly, in the book *Hair Story: Untangling the Roots of Black Hair in America*, authors Ayana D. Byrd, and Lori Tharps note that the terms "good hair" and "bad hair" came out of slavery. Black slaves who had features associated with mixed progeny (i.e., wavy or straight hair) would have better access to food, clothes, education, protection, and have a higher chance of being set free (26). For slaves, "good hair" literally meant a (comparatively) good life. African Americans' internalization of this white supremacist racial classification has brought about a society in which blacks are compelled to assimilate to be accepted. In essence, blacks have to force their hair to do something it does not do naturally: they must straighten out their kinks and curls. However, the process of hair straightening for blacks is complicated, time-consuming, and expensive. Thus, the willingness and unwillingness to wear one's black hair naturally has much to do with one's own views of the historical and contemporary valuations of hair that then influence these contemporary decisions.

During the 1960s and 1970s, the practice of hair straightening amongst women in the black community was fiercely contested. Prior to this, Patton suggests, the practice was viewed as "a pitiful attempt to emulate Whites and equated hair straightening with self-hatred and shame," yet with the dawning of the Black Power Movement, the afro was understood to denote black pride, a symbolic proclamation that "Black is Beautiful!" (29). The idea that black is not beautiful stemmed from the white standard of beauty that thus resulted in blacks' hair-straightening practice. Patton further examines blacks who went against such hair straightening practices such as W.E.B. DuBois, Booker T. Washington, and Malcolm X often wore out their afros or "natural hair" to contest the idea that black hair is slave hair and thus neither beautiful nor free; however, many black women felt straightened hairstyles were not about emulating whites but having a modern hairstyle (29). They also believed straightening one's hair is not synonymous with racial shame or "acting white." However, because modern hair is influenced by its history and the hegemonic white standard of beauty, African American women unwittingly and problematically conformed themselves to attain "good hair." Many African American women demonstrate an unwillingness to wear their hair natural as it is not seen as beautiful. Instead, it is seen as a reflection of slavery days that will continue to challenge African American women's survival in America. Thus, many African American women choose to endure chemical treatments that remove the kinks and curls from their hair.

The reason many African American women perm or straighten their hair is that it is less time-consuming and less painful than dealing with their kinky hair. Styling natural kinky hair in a way deemed socially acceptable is often frustrating for black women (Byrd and Tharps 149). Hence, dealing with straight and softer hair is easier than dealing with these women's kinky, curly, wool-like hair. Theresa Singleton, author of "Facing the Challenges of a Public African-American Archaeology," noted one way to straighten out African American women's kinks and curls is by the use of the "hot comb": a steel comb that is heated over a stove fire (149). The steam enters each hair strand individually, allowing tightly coiled kinks to straighten out. Cheryl Thompson, author of "Black Women and Identity: What's Hair Got to Do With It?" further notes that the "hot comb" is useful in that it allows for a quick method of straightening, but once exposed to moisture, black hair reverts back to its natural state. Thus, only an estimated five percent of African Americans use a hot comb to straighten their hair (Byrd and Tharps 162). A more common way of straightening one's hair is the use of a chemical straightener, also known as a "relaxer" or "creamy crack." Over sixty percent of African American women use this method to relax their hair (Byrd and Tharps 162). It was promoted as a less damaging product to the hair and scalp (Thompson). Chemical relaxers are also viewed as a more efficient way to straighten one's hair as it could be applied at home, does not require heat to maintain its effect, requires re-application only every two to three months and when wet, does not revert back to its natural puffy state but rather looks wet and straight.

However, chemically straightening one's hair can have many negative side effects. Dr. Dina Strachan, a New York City board certified dermatologist, states African American women who chemically treat their hair tend to have more brittle and fragile hair (Thompson). This alteration of hair texture increases the fragility of the hair cuticle and thus reduces the hair's ability to protect itself from damage. Dr. Strachan received many complaints, mostly from her African American patients, about their lack of hair growth, breakage, and hair loss. Chemically treating one's hair is a main cause of this. Relaxers are not "gentle hair care" and thus can dry out one's hair and cause damage that makes the hair break (Thompson). Users of relaxers are advised to constantly moisturize hair with oils and conditioner to lessen the damaging effects of chemicals on the hair. Why go through all this trouble to engage with society only to have unhealthy hair in the end? While the reasons are both problematic and multifarious, the answer lies partly in the struggle for employment.

The need for such an image causes African American women to spend more money on hair products than any cultural group in America (Chapman 26). Even the hair product ads displayed on the television seem geared towards selling to African Americans. Words like "detangle," "remove your kinks today," and "you want softer, more manageable hair?" pull African Americans in to buy all these hair products. Many blacks seek a way to make their hair salon visits shorter and their hair more manageable. The unattainable Eurocentric standard of beauty is used by the cosmetic industry and fashion magazines to encourage all women influenced by westernized ideas of beauty that they need to indulge in consumer capitalism in order to feel good about themselves—specifically, coercing women to buy the company's products (Chapman 27). As a result, the average black woman spends $300–1,200 on their hair monthly (27). Intrinsically this expense is neither foolish nor worthwhile. These women should not have to spend so much time and money on their hair just to be accepted by society. And although it is understood that black hair is a window into African American women's being and becoming, African Americans have gained their right to express their hair freely (Jacobs-Huey 4). Black women in America are buying into the myth that they have to consume these expensive hair products and do certain things to their hair to attain a standard of beauty defined in opposition to blackness. There is no one definition of beautiful, and thus blacks must embrace their natural beauty.

As noted above, for most African American women, natural hair is just simply unmanageable. Michele Chapman, author of "Black Women's Transformative Experience in their Self Perceptions of Abroad and at Home," states even women who do not chemically or thermally straighten their hair usually wear afros or dreadlocks, which are not originally natural in that they are controlled hairstyles (23). However, these controlled hairstyles are not seen as an appropriate style option. If black hair is not straight, it is seen as unprofessional or undesirable. To many whites in the United States, the afro style is intimidating because it has become a symbol of independence, resistance against white supremacy, and an assertion of black self-pride (69). In the workplace, African American women have to make a crucial decision to be natural or not. The afro is often seen as a distraction in the workplace, evidenced in an interview Chapman conducted with a woman named Sue who worked as an accountant in a professional setting. Sue stated that her afro was an integral part of her identity, yet her white co-workers thought the afro was "too out there" and that it should be "neater" (69). Thus, Sue decided to cut it off and get it permed. Sue noted she felt "corporate America" ultimately forced her to get rid of it. The way Sue chose to wear her hair had significant effects on her employment situation, suggesting not only challenges for presently employed blacks but also for job applicants choosing to wear their hair "natural." Sue's experience represents an even greater idea that hair in the black community is crucial to survival. This example, which anecdotal evidence suggests is a common occurrence, represents the ways black hair is viewed in the work force and how individuals are pressured to tame their hair in order to meet the white standard of professionalism and beauty.

However common these scenarios may be, evidence suggests that African American's views and perceptions toward natural hair has changed. In an article entitled "Natural Hair and the Workforce," author Desire Cooper notes more and more African-American women are going natural and saying goodbye to chemical hair relaxers. In 2011, the number of black women who said they did not use products to chemically relax or straighten their hair jumped to 36 percent, a 10 percent increase over the previous year, according to a report by Mintel, a consumer spending and market research firm (Cooper). Yet this growing number of women who stopped chemically treating their hair has seemingly been affected by workplace dynamics. For many black women, their urge to go natural is overshadowed by the fear that they will not be accepted or promoted at work (Cooper). In 2007, an editor at *Glamour* magazine declared that afros were a "no-no" in the workplace and that dreadlocks were "inappropriate" (Cooper). This idea that black natural hair does not get one very far still, unfortunately, seems very true. Historically, meeting white standards of beauty was needed to survive, but the same values and assumptions still hold true today. Author bell hooks, winner of the National Book Award and influential critic of race, gender and politics, has suggested "The first body issue that affects Black female identity, even more so than color, is hair texture. Certainly, going out to work in a White world that has always been threatened by Black people who appear to be decolonized, has had a major impact on what Black females choose to do with our hair." Hooks hones in on the central idea of a racially underpinned hierarchy of beauty blacks must meet immediately upon entering the work force. Simply put, black women cannot be themselves and sustain professional employment in most fields. The freedom to do what they please with their hair is threatened by their social and political survival. Ingrid Banks, author of *Hair Matters: Beauty, Power, and Black Women's Consciousness*, has furthermore noted that hair has become a marker of difference that black women recognize at an early age, particularly given the media representation of what constitutes beauty (23).

Black women face many pressures because of this white standard. In order to be a good-looking woman, according to the media and other means whereby the white standard of beauty is normalized, black hair is an accessory that just does not fit. Thus, black women who wear their hair naturally or "puffy" have somehow failed. Even in the black magazines such as *Essence* and *Ebony* one will see curly or straight hair as the dominant style. It is as though the media is conveying black is not beautiful in its entirety. Instead of black-owned media sources portraying what is known for black hair (kinky curly, and tightly coiled) in their magazines marketed to blacks, they are supporting the European standards of beauty by displaying the "loose-waved" or "straight" hair look on black women, equating beauty and success with "good hair."

This ambivalence has created a divide within the black community. Black women who adopt that standard of hair depicted in the black magazines do so possibly to gain more chances to get ahead of the black women with "nappy" hair. Evidently, the media's perception of beauty has added to both intragroup divisions and preexisting class divisions. The blue-eyed, blonde, thin white women is only as "beautiful" as she is because of a stark comparison to black women with classical African features of dark skin, full lips, and kinky hair (Chapman 25). Once a black woman chemically relaxes her hair, she somehow becomes beautiful—she becomes human. For black women, their hair is their identity, and media reinforces this point constantly. On the contrary, soul singer India.Arie's 2006 song "I Am Not My Hair" makes it clear otherwise. Her lyrics read "I am not my hair, I am not this skin / I am not your expectations no no/ I am a soul that lives within." This idea of breaking loose from the hegemonic standards of beauty seem to be running through the black community. And at some point when it was used powerfully in history to denote ethnic pride, it was not "bad" hair: it was just a statement. The terms "good" hair and "bad" hair should be eliminated from the consciousness of the black community because all hair is good hair as long as it is healthy. The effect the media has had on black women, however, has caused black women to think they are not beautiful. But like India.Arie's song conveys, beauty is what one makes of it.

As I have argued so far, the idea that hair is just a commodity without self-definition does seem true for some black women, yet black women address this issue in various ways. As noted earlier, not all African American women straighten their hair as a means of assimilation. Patton noted many black women straightened their hair to keep up with what is "modern" hair styling (29). Others, as suggested by Lanita Jacobs-Huey, author of *From the Kitchen to the Parlor: Language and African American Women's Hair Care*, straighten or relax their hair because they love the versatility of black hair.

They can get their hair to look like "cotton" one week and "bone straight" the other (Jacobs-Huey 112). This is dissimilar from white hair that is too soft to stay up in an afro style or to be braided or dreaded. As long as hair is tamed and neatly done, all hair can be seen as beautiful, even the afro. Nevertheless, because present-day society is still shaped by its historic values, the way one chooses to wear their hair has consequences. Hair could never and will never be just hair for the black community. After all, one does not see anyone in high positions of social prestige with natural hair (Cooper). In order to gain the respect needed for social advancement, many blacks have and will continue to emulate white hairstyles.

To illustrate how white standards continue to dominate questions of professionalism and beauty surrounding "good hair," President Obama's eleven-year-old daughter Malia wore her hair in twists while in Rome for the summer of 2009. Catherine Saint Louis, author of "Black Hair, Still Tangled in Politics," reports how commentators, especially those on the conservative blog Free Republic, attacked Malia as unfit to represent America on account of her appearance. This example shows that for young black girls, particularly the president's daughter, hair is important on symbolic levels. Hair has the power to dictate how others treat them, and in turn how they feel about themselves (Thompson). It is made clear from these recent attacks on Malia's natural hairstyle that the power of hair in the black community is still alive. The fact that the First Lady Michelle Obama, a prominent figure in the black community, straightens her hair also denotes how much weight hair holds in American society. Based on the response to Malia's hair, should the first lady have chosen to wear her hair naturally, the ample respect that she has gained from many white Americans would have been squandered. And according to these commentators, the Obama ladies should all have straight hair because that is what is associated with a "free-person's" status, as well as higher class ranking. Such instances of white standards being implicated on the first black president and his family are a large problem. The only way to fix such problems is to change the mindset of those who believe straight hair signifies beauty, wealth, and normalcy. In the meantime, the unwillingness of the Obama ladies to wear their hair naturally proves a prolonged image of straight hair that will continue to aid black women's social survival—but at a cost.

Hair has always been an important physical attribute for women because it is very visible and public (Banks 12). Understanding the importance of hair in the black community is to understand how, for black women, social survival means adopting an unrealistic standard of beauty and the concomitant financial and psychological burden—something most women never need to consider. During the Black Power Movement, many blacks were happy to wear their natural hair as it signified change and challenging the pre-set standards of beauty. As black women progress in the present day, more of them are beginning to embrace natural styles that emphasize the unique texture of their hair rather than trying to hide it (Byrd and Tharps 170). This does not go to say that many black women, including Michelle Obama, do not find more comfort in straightening their hair—chemically or thermally, due to their social status, or in regards to their employment. Nonetheless, this racially underpinned hierarchy of beauty seems set in stone. And because race is already very visual, and will always be a factor, it is rather necessary to raise a race consciousness among whites, both those who don't consider themselves racist yet benefit from existing power structures at the expense of others, and those who are bluntly racist need to be made aware of the destruction of blacks. Blacks are at a constant internal battle with themselves as they decide whether or not to defy or stand with the white European preset standards. As argued, there is black or there is white; there is no medium of gray. Thus, a greater consciousness in America is needed in order to move forward as one of the major world powers.

Works Cited

Banks, Ingrid. *Hair Matters: Beauty, Power, and Black Women's Consciousness*. New York: New York University, 2000. Print.

Bellinger, Whitney. "Why African American Women Try to Obtain 'Good Hair.'" *Sociological Viewpoints* 23 (2007): 63–72. *JSTOR*. Web. 26 Mar. 2014.

Byrd, Ayana D. & Tharps, Lori L. *Hair Story: Untangling the Roots of Black Hair in America*. New York: St. Martin's Press. 2001. Print.

Chapman, Yolanda Michele, "'I Am Not My Hair! Or Am I?': Black Women's Transformative Experience in their Self Perceptions of Abroad and at Home" (2007). *Anthropology Thesis*. Paper 23. Web. 30 Mar. 2014.

Cooper, Desiree. "Natural Hair and the Workforce." BLAC Detroit: Nov. 2013. Web. 27 Apr. 2014.

hooks, bell. *Sisters of the Yam: Black Women and Self-Recovery*. New York: South End Press, 2005. Print.

India.Arie. "I Am Not My Hair." *Testimony: Volume I*. Motown Records, 2006. MP3 file.

Jacobs-Huey, Lanita. *From the Kitchen to the Parlor: Language and Becoming in African American Women's Hair Care*. New York: Oxford University Press, 2006. Print.

Louis, Catherine Saint. "Black Hair, Still Tangled in Politics." *New York Times*. New York Times, 26 Aug. 2009. Web. 27 Apr. 2014.

Patton, Tracey Owens. "Hey Girl, Am I More than My Hair?: African American Women and Their Struggles with Beauty, Body Image, and Hair." *NWSA Journal* 18.2 (2006): 26–30. *JSTOR*. Web. 26 Mar. 2014.

Singleton, Theresa A. "Facing the Challenges of a Public African-American Archaeology." *Historical Archaeology* 31. 3 (1997): 146–52. *JSTOR*. Web. 9 Apr. 2014.

Thompson, Cheryl. "Black Women and Identity: What's Hair Got to Do With It?" *Michigan Feminist Studies* 22.1 (2008–2009). Web. 26 Mar. 2014.

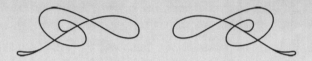

JiaJun Zou

JiaJun is the first in his family to attend college. He grew up in the United States as an immigrant from China who could speak very little English. Still, he dreams of one day becoming a History professor at Harvard University. His philosophy on writing is that writing is a process of brainstorming and constant revision. He believes that constructive criticism is what helps to shape a good essay.

Writing this essay was very difficult for JiaJun. He felt alienated from his peers and audiences due to the sensitivity of the topic. However, JiaJun made the commitment to exercise his writing skill to convey to others a sense of necessity for greater public attention on the crucial and prevalent issue that he is writing about. JiaJun enjoyed most the processing of piles of scholarly sources, carefully analyzing them, and putting them into a coherent piece of work. He revised his essay by attending Professor Angie Pelekidis' office hours several times and reading *They Say I Say* for advice.

JiaJun learned so much from both Writing 110 and Writing 111. He believes Writing 110 prepared him for college-level writing, and Writing 111 took a step further by improving his critical thinking skills and organization skills. Professor Pelekidis gave him great help with regard to coming up with writing ideas and proposing a reachable solution.

JiaJun's advice for future students: Take constructive criticism seriously and be grateful for it. No matter what you write, write with all your heart.

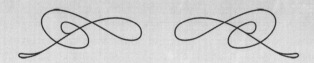

PROMOTING RACIAL AWARENESS: AN END TO COLOR-BLIND RACISM

JiaJun Zou

Professor Angie Pelekidis

While few people in the United States today would disagree that race still plays a big role in people's lives, it has gradually become a subject that many white Americans have become reluctant to discuss or recognize. This hesitation to recognize race, and thus racism, is known as Color-Blind Racism, or CBR, which can be found in rhetoric like "people of color, we don't see you (at least not that bad 'colored' part)" (Williams). The lack of awareness of race on the part of white Americans, the historical and institutional dominant group, often contributes to their passive attitude toward solving race-related issues. It is because of the perception that race no longer matters that racism is considered a phenomenon of the past. Although some would argue that the strategy of CBR reflects the intent of the dominant group to perpetuate white privilege and racism, my paper attempts to offer an alternative view by suggesting that the reproduction of CBR is largely a result of white Americans today having an inherent disadvantage in seeing racism as an evolving social issue. This inherent disadvantage stems from factors such as a lack of racial awareness, conditioned by the context of social environments; a lack of perceived necessity to be concerned about race as a life-affecting issue; and the culture of believing that blindness to race can foster positive harmony between individuals of different races.

These causes of white Americans' colorblind mindsets help to produce a vicious cycle in which the well-intentioned idea to end racism through racial blindness functions within the context of a society of growing racism, which is a system that includes racial inequality, injustice, prejudice, stereotypes, discrimination, and institutional racism. Within this context, the dominant group can perpetuate racism by allowing it to go unacknowledged. My paper attempts to explain how a mindset that fosters CBR is formed in early child-hood for many young whites, and how it systematically exacerbates racism regardless of their wills to participate. Thus, my paper differs from the con-ventional view on CBR being a strategy of the dominant group for self-in-terest. I see it as instead as a product of white Americans' growing up with disadvantages that made race and racism invisible, and thus contribute to their failure of solving racism, with the inadvertent consequence of perpetu-ating racism. In response to the problem of CBR, my paper proposes two educational reforms to nourish and cultivate positive racial awareness in early childhood. First, I propose a K–12 race-related curriculum to remediate the lack of racial knowledge and awareness among young American students, especially children of the dominant group who were raised to be colorblind. Second, I propose extending multicultural curriculums to teachers' educa-tion to enhance their activism in conducting multicultural discourse and thus forming a race-conscious perspective of their students in an early age. These two reforms are predicted to be mutually reinforcing to improve racial aware-ness in students and would encourage their propensity to take public action against racism in the long run. They also serve as a way to control and elimi-nate the potential reproduction of racist ideas that can easily be developed in children who live colorblind lives, as my paper will prove that CBR is detrimental to a multiracial society as a whole.

While colorblindness is often considered a positive approach to race by the dominant group, it alienates white Americans from minorities due to the fact that it fosters negative racialized attitudes, especially among young whites whose idea of race can be tainted by social environments and underpinned by negative, misguided information. Furthermore, CBR rejects the fact that mi-norities today continue to face various forms and levels of racism and evades any responsibility of the dominant group for the racial status quo. Monica Williams, PhD, in her recent publication in *Psychology Today*, suggests that white Americans' colorblindness "creates a society that denies their [minori-ties'] negative racial experiences, rejects their [minorities'] cultural heritage, and invalidates their [minorities'] unique perspectives" (Williams). Williams argues that "research [by D. S Holoien] has shown that hearing colorblind messages predicts negative outcomes among whites, such as greater racial bias and negative affect…[and] causes stress in ethnic minorities, resulting in decreased cognitive performance" (qtd. in Williams). In other words, the avoidance strategy of CBR proves detrimental toward creating a society in which race doesn't matter, but rather help to shape the chasm across which white Americans and minorities live in racially stratified and mutually dis-connected lives. Williams's concern about minorities facing a denial of their experience and white Americans developing a tendency to racial bias shows the contradiction between CBR's intended purpose and expected result. The problem here lies in the way colorblind ideology makes the assumption that race no longer matter and racism no longer exists.

It is true that Colorblind ideology can be an appealing ideal on the surface to many white Americans. It creates a common ground with minorities, which is the common goal of living in a society where race and racism no longer affect people's lives, showing that most whites and minorities desire racial equality and an elimination of racism. However, its essence is deceiving and misleading. CBR approaches racism, which is a system of various ways of oppression and stratification, by assuming that they no longer exist or dismissing the whole idea that race exists in a social context rather than actively collaborating with minorities to combat racism in both personal and institutional levels. In order to see the dismissal and denial caused by CBR in action, one need to first look at how CBR is instilled in young American whites. According to a 2012 study by Michael I. Norton, an associate professor at Harvard Business School, which was cited in Harvard University Newsletter *Working Knowledge*, experiments showed that whites as young as ten have adopted the CBR strategy of avoiding racial recognition when they were asked to identify minorities (qtd. in Nobel). One plausible explanation to this situation is that young whites " 'get the message that they are not supposed to acknowledge that they notice people's race—often the result of a horrified reaction from a parent when they do' " (qtd. in Nobel). This context indicates that it wasn't because young whites have an innate difficulty or inability to recognize race, but rather race has been made invisible to them at a young age. This is significant in building up colorblindness for young whites whose ability to perceive race and racism has been shaped and constrained by the beliefs of their parents. Since children will grow up to be citizens and policy-makers, their environment is important to the ideals they'll develop. In addition to the parents' own beliefs, the instilment of colorblind mindsets by parents in young whites also depends on the social environment in which these parents helped to create for their children.

As Norton had suggested earlier, the study by Margaret Ann Hagerman, a PhD Candidate in the Department of Sociology at Emory University, confirms that white parents often contribute positively or negatively to the development of racial awareness in their children, depending on how they choose to interpret race and racism to their children (Hagerman 1). Hagerman conducted research on two sets of white American households, one colorblind and the other with racial awareness, meaning aware of the impact of race and racism in our society. The research shows how the two ideologies can produce different outcomes of children growing up viewing race and racism differently. Hagerman's study found that white parents who exposed their children to a social environment comprised of predominantly white neighborhoods and schools, and to socialize and interact with predominantly white people, more often create unfavorable effects in their children's development of racial awareness than the white parents who do otherwise (Hagerman 8). Her research found that "these parents construct a colour-blind racial context of childhood in which race is a 'non-issue' once the context in constructed" (Hagerman 8). At the age of 11 and 12, these children had little or no opportunity to interact with minorities or to learn about minorities' racialized experience through education (Hagerman 11). Like the research by Williams and Norton, which suggested a possible reproduction of racial bias through CBR, Hagerman's study agrees that the young whites who grew up within the context of CBR can develop their racial understanding out of narrow information and thus become racially biased (Hagerman 11). Thus, Hagerman suggests that children have the ability to perceive race but often when they do, it was with little sense of connection to their own experience, given that they grew up in a racially segregated environment. This is not to imply that young whites were more likely to develop bias themselves but rather to reveal the logic of how CBR served as a counterproductive strategy toward reaching the common goal of all races being socially equal. Moreover, the example proves that parents' good intentions to enforce a colorblind mindset can inadvertently expose young whites to a social context in which racist rhetoric and beliefs are easily circulated through social media and compounded by public apathy. This tendency to be influenced by negative racial beliefs can be seen in Hagerman's interviews with colorblind young whites who felt "black equals getting in trouble" or "Mexican immigrants were lazy and came here to steal our jobs and money" (Hagerman 12). The biases and stereotypes as shown in these children's descriptions of blacks and Mexicans contradict the parents' intention to help shape a society within which race doesn't matter. Thus, it shows that CBR perpetuates racism by giving young whites a disadvantage in seeing racism as an evolving issue, but rather preparing them for racism by taking away their opportunity to interact with and learn from minorities about their racialized experience.

Moreover, the same research suggested that white parents who raised their children in racially diverse neighborhoods, exposed them to racially diverse schools, and encouraged their racial awareness through conversations on race contributed to their children's positive racial understanding (Hagerman 8). Not only were these young children receptive to the concept of white privilege, but they also believed that the fear of recognizing race and racism is still a big problem today (Hagerman11). Lindsey, a brave ten-year-old white girl, unlike her peers, didn't believe that race doesn't matter today: "My third grade teacher was racist. She kept making fun of this one kid who was my friend Ronnie. He's my buddy…he didn't really do well in school. She would hold up his work and then make fun of it in front of the whole class. And she would yell at him. She only did that kind of thing to that race!" (Hagerman 12). Lindsey also sadly and angrily told the story of her black classmates who waited for a bus that never made it to their neighborhood; they walked to school in wet clothing and were punished for lateness. As a result, Lindsey and her parents took immediate action to stop and prevent further racist actions against her minority peers (Hagerman 12). This contrast with the previous example, which shows how colorblind young whites view blacks as "equal to trouble," proves that young whites who were raised in the context of racial awareness have the advantage of seeing racism as an evolving issue and often felt a sense of responsibility for action rather than leaning toward retreat and passivity. Hagerman concludes that children's agency to think critically about race and racism can be "reworked rather than reproduced, which has significant implications for launching challenges against the racial status quo" (Hagerman 14). In other words, white children who grow up within the context of racial awareness can better serve the goal of ending racism because they are more likely to recognize the problem, and thus address it, than young whites whose experiences with racial awareness had been limited by their parents and environments. In other words, white children who grow up within the context of CBR have an inherent disadvantage in recognizing racism as an evolving issue, and are more likely to produce inherent racial bias, given the limited race-related education or interracial experience. This makes them susceptible to the negative influence of social media and racialized images pinned to different minorities (e.g., "blacks equal trouble"). The significance of developing racial awareness in early childhood is also important, given that Hagerman's research also suggests that early childhood development of racial understanding (either racial awareness or colorblindness) often lasts throughout life. (Hagerman 14).

My paper proposes that the first step toward eliminating CBR is to develop racial awareness in children through establishing race-related curriculum in K–12 education. Although Hagerman's research suggested that parents and neighborhoods often had an impact in shaping the racial perspective of young whites, it also implied that children have the agency to learn and to formulate their own understanding of race by reaching out of their comfort zone and developing a shared understanding of race with their minority peers, as we see in Lindsey's case above. Thus, it suggests that an extension of opportunity to learn about race-related curriculum can remediate the lack of racial awareness in the context of CBR at home. Furthermore, race-related curriculums have already been proven effective in improving racial awareness by various studies.

One of these studies, conducted by Timothy D. Levonyan Radloff, Ph.D., an assistant professor of Sociology at SUNY Fredonia, shows that white college students had improved their racial attitudes toward minorities after they completed multiple race-related courses. Moreover, Radloff's research found that efforts to "diversify the curriculum have contributed to a positive change in racial attitudes and commitment to improving racial understanding." One example he gave was that, despite studies indicating most white students to be initially resentful of Affirmative Action policy, which intended to help students from historically underrepresented groups, "modern racism was not only lower in students who fulfilled the university's diversity requirement for graduation, but these students were also more likely to support race-based policy" (Radloff). In order words, education has proven to change students' perception of race by allowing them to enrich their knowledge through education, helping them to become less confined to their social circle in which information comes primarily from parents or social media.

Despite the effectiveness of this method of using education to fight CBR, courses like Sociology and Human Development, which often include race-related teachings, are not common in K–12 education. For example, Michael DeCesare, Ph.D., an associate professor at Merrimack College, points out that "sociology courses have been offered at the college level since at least 1876.... [And] now exist in just about every college curriculum" (Decesare 211). Nonetheless, only 23 percent of high schools in the greater Sacramento area of California offered at least one sociology course; 24 percent in New York; 52 percent in Pennsylvania; 68 percent in Connecticut (Decesare 212). Decesare concludes that the substantial challenge is that the decision whether Sociology should be taught in high school is always determined by individual schools (Decesare 214). The statistic shows that over the years, little attention has been given by school officials on the practical and moral necessity for nourishing racial awareness in their students. Thus, my paper argues that race-related curriculums should be extended to K–12 educational levels because they represent a substantial improvement for addressing the issue of CBR.

Moreover, in addition to Radloff's study, there is another evidence that shows how college-level teaching on race and racism provides a process of learning that overcomes the existing color-blind mindsets among white students, and even prompts them to take responsibility into their own hands. According to research on race-related curriculums in college by Kathleen J. Martin, a Ph.D. of ethnic studies at the University of California, despite "students' personal beliefs and attitudes that were often in opposition to course materials and faculty knowledge," educational experience promotes "cognitive (intellectual functioning) and affective (feelings and beliefs) learnings" that often enable students to "increase their knowledge and awareness as active learners; thereby taking responsibility for their learning" (Martin). Her research suggests that this process of promoting racial awareness in higher education was able to encourage students to connect abstract theories on books to real world practices (Martin). In other words, white college students not only learned about racism in the classroom, they were also able to utilize course knowledge to address serious concerns related to racism in society today, further indicating the correlation between introducing race-related curriculum and improving racial awareness. Similarly, this idea of connecting racial awareness to taking action against the racial status quo was exemplified in the earlier example of Lindsey, the ten-year-old white girl who, with her parents, came to the defense of her friend Ronnie. Thus, it shows that an awareness of racism can prompt immediate action toward stopping racism, whereas blindness toward racism makes racism invisible and irrelevant. From the example of college level race-related curriculum, we can infer that K–12 level race-related courses aiming to develop racial awareness can also be equally effective.

Although some readers may object that it would be naive to expect young children in K–12 education level to have the same ability as college students to learn about race and racism, this paper would answer that as shown in the aforementioned studies, children can improve their racial awareness themselves once they are exposed to a variety of information that challenges their conceptual understanding of race. Likewise, as suggested by Radloff and Martin, a college student was also able to improve racial awareness only after being exposed to race-related materials in the classroom. This similarity of outcome demonstrates that age does not impair young whites' ability to learn about race and race-related materials. The curriculum would allow young whites to bridge the chasm of racial understanding and racial experience. Thus, the reasoning here shows that extending race-related curriculum to young whites at an early age is a feasible alternative for the cause of promoting racial awareness and ending racism.

However, the concern regarding how young whites can improve their racial awareness through education requires teachers with more racial knowledge. Therefore, the second concrete step to be taken would be to extend race-related education to teachers in order to improve the racial awareness and knowledge of their students. Recent research conducted by Gloria Boutte, Julia Lopez-Robertson, and Elizabeth Powers-Costello, published in *Early Childhood Education Journal*, illustrates the predominance of colorblind mindsets in teachers of early education. As the research suggests, "the reality that the vast majority of educators do not intentionally commit acts of racism does not negate the fact that anybody can contribute to institutional racism unless efforts are taken to avoid doing so" (335). Thus, CBR could be practiced unknowingly by many well-intentioned teachers committed to the idea that it is enough to think race doesn't matter in a social context. The intentional avoidance and the lack of motivation to engage students in race-related conversation and learning about race were both detrimental to the development of racial awareness. Despite reluctance on the teachers' parts to introduce conversations about race, the children themselves were eager to participate when engaged, given that colorblindness was less deep-rooted at an early age and had to be taught in order to suppress racial awareness. Their research discovered that asking young children to express their ideas of racism through arts and drawing or class discussion shows positive outcome of racial awareness, implying that colorblind mindsets have to be taught consistently in order to be embedded in the minds of children (338). In response to the previous studies given in this paper, it also affirms that "early childhood years are important for interrupting racism and make suggestions for helping children develop tools for addressing it" (335).

Nonetheless, the study extends beyond the idea that most teachers simply did not desire race conversation as it suggests that it was because most teachers were unfamiliar with the race-related concepts and knowledge (Boutte, Robertson, Castillo 335). In effect, if a teacher recognizes that "silence on these issues contributes to the problem, then they may be more likely to interrupt racism rather than ignore it" (335). The research implies that teachers shouldn't refrain from discussing and interpreting race-related issue with young children. Teachers' active participation in helping young children to understand and to address race and racism was "both an educational and ethical necessity" (335).This is because teachers also play a similar role to parents since they both have the ability and opportunity to shape the racial awareness of young children. Furthermore, the research found that children's drawings and dialogues not only reflected their shared understanding of racism but further indicated their ability to perceive the prevalence of racism minorities face in a daily life (Boutte, Robertson, Castillo 335).

Thus, this study shows again that children often have the agency to perceive racism more objectively and directly than adults, proving that CBR was less of an idea inherent to young whites but more of a constructed idea that young whites developed in the context of lacking racial knowledge and racial awareness. This childhood insight on race and racism reveals that children have the capacity and interest to learn about these issues, and their racial awareness can be properly nourished once they received a race-related curriculum, which I proposed earlier. On the other hand, the counterargument that children in K–12 education level are too young to learn about racial reality underestimates children's ability, exposes them to the sole influence of a colorblind mindset at home, and precludes their opportunity to develop an awareness on race themselves with the help of education. This is not to say that white parents don't have the responsibility for young whites' development of racial awareness, but rather to emphasize that teachers can be an alternative source of help in providing racial awareness to young whites. We can also extrapolate that if children have the capacity to learn and to understand racism through the light of education, there can be a possibility for them to address CBR at home, thereby changing the color-blind mindsets of their parents.

Colorblind racism, which appears to be an ideal response toward growing racism in the United States today has proven to be a passive and counterproductive response on the part of the dominant group, the white Americans. Although it is true that a colorblind attitude can also be adopted by some minorities, the dominant group remains the one that receives institutional privileges based on race and exempted from systematic oppression based on race. With compelling evidence, this paper debunks CBR as an idea that makes the mistakes of assuming race doesn't matter in a social context, and so action is unnecessary, and that blindness toward race and racism can lead to their disappearance. A colorblind attitude gives longevity to racism by covering up the imperfect and racialized society in which we reside. Despite the prevalence of CBR, my paper conveys the hope that young whites who grow up in the context of racial awareness have the potential to push for racial equality and an end to color-blind racism. My paper refutes the myth that colorblindness is a positive strategy toward solving the racial problem today, and calls for two specific educational reforms in an effort to promote racial awareness: the introduction of race-related curriculum in early education, and greater multicultural education for teachers—who are often the role models for their students in the same way that parents are to their children—in order to allow them to foster positive racial mindsets in their students. The wound will not be healed unless it is seen, and racism will not be gone unless it is found.

Works Cited

Boutte, Gloria, Julia Lopez-Robertson, and Elizabeth Powers-Costello. "Moving Beyond Colorblindness in Early Childhood Classrooms." *Early Childhood Education Journal* 39.5 (2011): 335–342. *Professional Development Collection*. Web. 8 May 2014.

DeCesare, Michael. "What Determines Whether Sociology is Taught in High School?" *Michigan Sociological Review* 20 (2006): 211–229. Web. 8 May 2014.

Hagerman, Margaret Ann. "White Families and Race: Colour-Blind and Colour-Conscious Approaches to White Racial Socialization." *Ethnic and Racial Studies* (2008): 1–16. 21 Web. 8 May 2014.

Ingersoll, Richard M. May. "The Minority Teacher Shortage: Fact or Fable?" *Phi Delta Kappan*. Sept. 1, 2011, 62–64. Web. 8 May 2014.

Martin, Kathleen J. "Student Attitudes and the Teaching and Learning of Race, Culture And Politics." *Teaching and Teacher Education* 26 (2010): 530–539. Web. 8 May 2014.

Nobel, Carmen. "The Case Against Racial Colorblindness." *Working Knowledge*. Harvard Business School. 13 Feb. 2012. Web. 8 May 2014.

Radloff, Timothy D. Levonyan. "College Students' Perceptions Of Equal Opportunity For African Americans And Race-Based Policy: Do Diversity Course Requirements Make A Difference?" *College Student Journal* 44.2 (2010): 558–564. *Professional Development Collection*. Web. 8 May 2014.

Williams, Monica. "Colorblind Ideology is a Form of Racism." *Psychology Today*. 27 Dec. 2011. Web. 8 May 2014.

WRITING 110
ESSAY

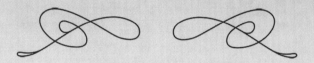

Mariam Traore

Writing 110 is a class that Educational Opportunity Program and Academic Success Program students take in the fall semester of their first year. The course prepares them for the rigors of college writing and focuses on the development of personal authority and agency through writing.

Mariam Traore's assignment was to write a narrative illustrating how she got into college, imagining as her readers high school students who need inspiration to work harder or to apply to college. Her goal was to persuade the reader without being intimidating. She writes:

> As a student who struggled in high school, encouraging stories made me want to strive for more. I wrote my piece to be honest, vivid, and relatable. Thinking back to the students in my high school, we all had a similar experience and the bullying I experienced is something most students go through. I was hoping to show that it shouldn't stop students from succeeding, but provide motivation to do better. I wanted my essay to be a mix of informal and formal language. Personally, I enjoy authentic informal language because it allows me to relate more…. And I wanted to challenge myself by writing two narratives that connect with each other.

Mariam's essay "Trespasser" won the Writing Initiative's Prize for the best Writing 110 essay of Fall 2014. We are proud to publish it in *Binghamton Writes*.

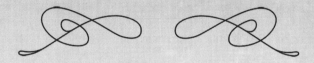

TRESPASSER

Mariam Traore

Professor Sean Fenty

Three blocks from home, I stood by this gray alleyway. Due to my cousin Alima's persistence and persuasion, I agreed to take a "short cut" with her. Even though this was supposed to be a short cut, it required me to jump over fences and run through dark tunnels. But not wanting to go home so soon, I decided to go with her. Summer was ending and I wanted to spend as much time with my cousin as possible, so we chose to head back slowly. It had rained earlier that day, which made the concrete moist and the air around us muggy. The deeper we got into the alleyway, the rustier it started to smell. We arrived at a shiny, newly placed fence, and I noticed it was about my adolescent height. My cousin and I clutched the shaky fence and steadily went over it. She played music loudly through her old Sidekick, even though it was late at night.

"C'mon turn it off, we don't even live in this building," I urged.

"Yo, I do this all the time. No one ever wakes up," Alima said.

Within seconds I heard: "You fucking trespassers, I'm going to get you!" A petite red-faced man waved his fist from the other side of the fence. Scared and puzzled, Alima and I ran for it. She sprinted in front of me, and all I could do was to listen for the heavy beats of her footsteps and her inconsistent breathing. My face was hot, my blood was boiling, and my heartbeats matched the slams of my worn-out Nikes on the pavement. I did not dare to turn around because I was petrified of what this madman could do. We arrived at a rusty brown fence. I hesitated to grab it because at this moment, I believed the fence was six stories high. I glanced at Alima's face. She had the most distressed look; however, holding on to hope, she got over the fence with ease. "C'mon we're almost there," she yelled to encourage me.

With my emotions in a frenzy, I pulled myself up, the fence coloring my hands black and brown. As I secured my small fingertips to the top of the fence and jerked myself up, I felt almost blissful, until I felt a pull on my leg, dragging me down from the fence. The red-faced man had a hold of my foot! "I'm calling the fucking police," he declared.

My heart sank and my mind went blank. *No! I can't get caught.* I kicked down to loosen his hold and went over the top of the fence, giving up on safety make it over. I held my heavy breath and jumped down. I hit the pavement, scraping my hands and ripping my jeans. My cousin grabbed my arm to lift me from the ground and we ran. "Never again," I vowed to myself as I sucked in the cold air, fisting my hands. I never wanted to feel that way again.

I broke that vow.

I was surrounded…surrounded by the smartest kids in my grade. Why the hell am I in this class? I quickly glanced at my neighbor's 97 on her math test and compared it to my 83. I slid my textbook to cover up my grade and used my hands to conceal the red marks on my paper. At that point, I had been in this small school for three months, and I masked my test grades every time I received them. Honestly, my grades were not that bad, but being around A+ students really made me feel bad.

My wrinkled, slow-talking math teacher would write a "Do-Now" on the board, and within seconds, hands would be raised. I never once put my hand up, but my teacher loved to pick on me. Doing as I was told, I got up, fixed my pleated gray skirt, put my hair behind my ear, and walked up to the board. When I was finished, my teacher would ask the students if the answer was correct. The majority of the time, I would hear a surround-sound "no," and he'd ask what did I do wrong. This made my blood boil, my face hot, and my heart beat too quickly for me to keep up with. The last thing I wanted was to have my failures known to all the smart kids in the class. Although the girls were nice, they were quick to talk about other students and discuss how deserving they were of being in honors classes. My biggest fear was that they would talk about me.

One dank winter morning, I went to school early to study for a test. Feeling the winter blues and not wanting to jump into work so soon, I decided to walk over to my friends' homerooms. Day-dreaming, I walked through the empty, narrow hallways, taking my time. It was quiet enough to hear noise coming from the classrooms down the hall. My ears suddenly focused when I heard my name. First, I thought someone was calling me. As I approached the noisy room, I heard my name again, followed by laughter.

"How did she even get into the class? She failed like three tests in math class! When she talks it doesn't even make sense!"

Hearing that felt like being punctured by a knife, and I did not want to hear any more. I started to see red, but I decided to calm myself down. I walked into the dimly-lit classroom, and it suddenly went quiet. The silence lasted a few moments; I glanced at them quickly, but only caught a teary-eyed blur of the black, gray, and white of our high school uniforms. Nevertheless, I put on a big smile and said, "hi," trying to hide my tears. They gave me a defiant look, and my mind finally went blank. It felt like that fateful night when the red-faced man grabbed me to pull me down. Trespasser. *Trespasser.* But unlike the first time, this time I was not in the wrong. I was not a fucking trespasser. I felt my soul blacken with thoughts of revenge. I deserve to be here like everyone else. They made me feel like I was an inferior, but I was *never* going to let that happen again.

From that point on, I worked harder. I may have not been a straight A student, but I worked hard and got the grades that I deserved. Although I dreaded raising my hand, I had to do it to prove to my teacher *and myself* that I understood the topics and problems at hand. The first time I volunteered for a "Do Now" problem, I surprised my teacher. He called on me, and I fixed my skirt, grabbed my notebook, and walked towards the board. Since my volunteering shocked people, I purposefully screeched the chalk across the boards. I heard a few groans, but I really did not care. I was focused on getting the answer right. When I was done I looked at the students' faces with a sense of satisfaction. My teacher asked if I had done it correctly, and I remember a couple of people saying, "yes," dejectedly.

When I received my test grades, I refused to cover my score, good or bad. I still got looks from these honor students, but I really did not care. However, it was satisfying when the snoopy girls looked at my score and it was higher than theirs. I gladly never heard my name come out of their mouths again.

Now, as I sit on my dorm room floor, reflecting on high school and listening to music, I am glad that those girls decided to talk about me. It motivated me to do more for myself. Even though anger was my motivation at first, it changed to self-satisfaction. To me, self-satisfaction is the most important attribute you can have, because you cannot be happy if you're not happy with yourself and your achievements. I learned throughout high school that satisfying *yourself* and doing better for *yourself* is the only way you can make it to college. All it required was a little hard work and dedication. With those, never again will anyone make me feel like a trespasser.